20/11/07 .

BLACKPOOL AND
THE FYLDE COLLEGE

7 DAY LOAN

This book must be returned to the College Resource Centre
on or before the last date stamped below

SITE SELECTION AND INVESTIGATION
A Practical Handbook

SITE SELECTION AND INVESTIGATION

A Practical Handbook

Edited by

**Dan Lampert
and
Douglas R Woodley**

Gower

Published by
Gower Publishing Company Limited
Gower House
Croft Road
Aldershot
Hants GU11 3HR
England

Gower Publishing Company
Old Post Road
Brookfield
Vermont 05036
USA

British Library Cataloguing in Publication Data
Site selection and investigation.
1. Construction. Sites. Investigation
I. Lampert, Dan II. Woodley, Douglas R.
690

Library of Congress Cataloguing-in-Publication Data
Site selection and investigation : a practical handbook / edited by
Dan Lampert and Douglas R. Woodley.
p. cm.
Includes index.
1. Building sites--Evaluation. 2. Real estate development.
I. Lampert, Dan, 1920– . II. Woodley, Douglas R.
HD1390.S59 1991
333.7'15--dc20   90–15506
                                                          CIP

ISBN 0 566 09090 2

Printed and bound in Great Britain by Billing & Sons Ltd, Worcester

Contents

Illustrations

Notes on Contributors

D.L. Barry, BE, CEng, MICE, MIHT, (Redevelopment of contaminated land) is head of Waste and Contaminated Land Division with W.S. Atkins Planning Consultants. He has been involved exclusively with contaminated land issues for more than ten years and leads a team of scientists, planners and engineers in the investigation, assessment and rehabilitation of former industrial and waste disposal sites. He lectures on the subjects of Contaminated Land and Landfill Gas problems.

C.R.I. Clayton, PhD, MSc, DIC, CEng, MICE (Recommendations for the procurement of ground investigation) is Reader in the Department of Civil Engineering at the University of Surrey.

Dr Martin E. Griffiths, BSc, DPhil, MIBiol, CBiol, (Constraints of the natural environment on site selection) is Senior Consultant, Appletree Environmental Consultancy. He is an independent environmental consultant specializing in the assessment of the ecological effects of development on natural communities. His experience ranges from advice to industry on the impact of pipelines and power stations and the appearance as expert witness at public inquiries to the survey of wildlife potential of areas of nature conservation interest for the Nature Conservancy Council, conservation education and the planning and development of nature reserves.

Dan Lampert, BSc (Eng), FICE, FIMech.E, FInstPet, (Editor, Initial investigations; Access and utilities; Appendix) is a project engineering consultant. He has had a lifetime experience of the survey for and construction of multidisciplinary projects; he is an advisor to an engineering management training school and lectures on site selection.

Denis F. McCoy, Dipl Arch(Oxford), ARIBA, MRIAI, FRTPI, McCoy Associates, (Obtaining planning permission) has been the Principal of an independent planning consultancy since 1980. He has dealt with conservation area studies and the promotion of environmental enhancements, the obtaining of planning consent, appeals and the provision of expert witnesses at inquiries. Previously he had seven years in the private sector on town and country development as well as eight years' experience in the public sector in England and in Ireland.

Neil T. Pepperell, Dip MBS (hons), GInstM, FBIM, (Professional indemnity insurance) is Managing Director of RIBA Indemnity Research Limited. He started as a Quantity Surveyor and has held several Directorships. In 1971 he was awarded the Institute of Marketing prize for Marketing. He is a member of the Society of Construction Law, the Architectural Association, the Comité de Liaison des Architectes, WIMLAS Advisory Board and BRE new DATA LINK project. He specializes in the discovery of the causes of building errors leading to insurance related claims against consultants.

Robert Andrew Robinson, FSVA, (Site selection for an industrial development) is Property Director of Kingston Estates and Managing Director of Kingston Estates (Management). He has been in the profession for the past 22 years and has been involved in all aspects of property, including both public and private sector. His main activities since the early 1970s have been in development, mainly commercial. At present he is working in the commercial development field but with some responsibility for residential development and the running of a building company.

Peter J. Smith, BSc, ARICS, Chartered Land Surveyor, (H.M. Land Registry) is Principal Survey and Plans Officer with H.M. Land Registry and has been a surveyor for over 30 years. He has been head of H.M. Mapping Division for the past 12 years dealing with disputes concerning registered boundaries.

D.J. Sweeney, BSc, MSc, CEng, MICE (Different types of foundation) is Technical Director, W.S. Atkins Consultants Limited. He has been a practising geotechnical engineer for more than 20 years and has dealt with foundation engineering problems in the UK, Hong Kong and USA. In Hong Kong he was a member of the Hong Kong Steering Committee dealing with the problems of constructing high-rise buildings on Hong Kong's steeply sloping landslide-prone ground.

J.F. Uff, QC, PhD, C Eng, FICE, FCIArb, MConsE (Recommendations for the procurement of ground investigation) is a consulting engineer, arbitrator and barrister at law specializing in construction law. He is also Visiting Professor in Civil Engineering at King's College, London.

Donald G. Valentine, MA (Cantab), LLB (Cantab), Dr Jur (Utrecht), FCI

Arb, (Comments on the Institution of Civil Engineers Conditions of Contract for Ground Investigation) is a barrister specializing in construction contracts. He often appears in court and in arbitrations in the UK and overseas.

Nicholas Maxwell White, ACII FCILA, (What happens when things go wrong) is a director of Toplis Construction, Chartered Loss Adjusters and Surveyors. He is also an independent consultant to Lloyds underwriters and insurance companies. He has 22 years' experience of dealing with claims arising from construction projects.

Douglas R Woodley, MEng, DSc (Editor) has for many years been internationally concerned with construction mechanization in Building and Civil Engineering contracts. He was editor of an encyclopedia of mechanical construction equipment which has become a 'bible' in the industry. He is currently involved in engineering management training.

Chapter 1

INITIAL INVESTIGATIONS

Dan Lampert

The decision to embark on a search for a suitable site implies the result of a predevelopment study which has confirmed the need. The search is therefore the start of an entrepreneurial venture or recognition of a requirement to meet a demand. The reasoning which lies behind the decision is that the new project will be of benefit to its promoter either industrially or socially. This study, possibly part of a viability study, should include an estimate of the following costs all of which are relevant to the selection of a property:

- the cost of the land
- surveyor's and legal fees
- the construction of the project including installation of machinery and equipment
- unit rates for utility consumption
- the cost of administration and operation of the project
- transportation of raw materials to site
- distribution costs from site
- maintenance
- taxation locally
- other capital and running costs.

The capital sum spread over a predetermined number of years plus the annual running cost for each of the years can then be compared with the revenue anticipated to ascertain whether there is sufficient profit to justify the choice of site.

If any of the above costs are underestimated, the true costs when known may indicate that the project is not viable. Costs envisaged need to be tabulated together with comments and conclusions in order that should hindsight prove the conclusion to be wrong the original reasoning will be available to explain why 'it seemed right at the time'.

The conceptual considerations for an industrial development include:

- is there a positive indication of a growing demand, e.g. as supported by market research?
- what possibilities are there to meet this demand, e.g. competitors working with the same idea?
- what throughput should the project have?
- is an expansion of throughput likely to be needed?
- is there a possibility of collapse of demand, e.g. a change in technology or the economy reducing the demand?

Having reviewed, decided and recorded conclusions the next subjects for consideration are:

- would the location of a project depend on its nearness to a source of raw materials or to a strategic location within the market for the product or to the availability of skilled labour for production?
- what is the ideal shape and ideal area of the property being sought?

If the presence of raw materials is critical to the choice of location then verification is needed to ensure:

- the provision of suitable material for the life of the project
- whether the price of the material will remain satisfactory and controllable.

The cost of transportation of raw materials and product may be the critical factor, in which case studies will be needed to compare the costs of transport by road, rail or possibly inland waterway. If the basic requirement is for skilled labour someone will have to decide whether a pool of labour currently available will continue. Businesses which were set up in the southeast of the UK to benefit from available labour are now facing a shortage of operational labour.

The time needed to carry out studies to select a site may take up to two years. If the nature of the industry is such that there could be objections and a public inquiry, an even longer period could be needed.

The first step

The owners of a proposed development normally assign a representative from their own staff or possibly an outside consultant to handle the project and decide on a site. The efficiency with which this task is accomplished will naturally depend on the competence of those involved. Companies which are continually expanding and seeking new sites retain their own permanent project teams. For the company which is in the market for a new site once every few years, it may be more practical to employ the services of a consultant, preferably one who knows the business, to work alongside one of the company managers who has been suitably briefed. This arrangement can also be of benefit if there is a need to keep the new project confidential until final decisions have to be made, as the consultant can do all the enquiring.

A project team for a major scheme could consist of:

- the team leader, preferably from the company
- an outside consultant, if the company owner so chooses
- a company representative who can speak for management, marketing and production
- a mechanical engineer if mechanical/process layout is involved
- an estimator
- a cost engineer familiar with financial aspects.

This team will need to deal with all the items listed at the beginning of this chapter and in addition design the layout of buildings, negotiate with local authorities, estate and land agents, obtain planning permissions, arrange meetings with prospective contractors, trade union officials, utility and transportation companies and possibly attend a public inquiry. The cost of this effort could be high and it is suggested that the team members keep time sheets to show how their time was spent. There are ways to reduce expenditure, for example, to undertake desk studies rather than to be on sites away from home, but much depends on how accurate the information needs to be. Expressed as a percentage of the total installed cost of the project a team for a small project could cost around 4 per cent of the total whereas a multimillion pound project team could cost around 0.3 per cent of total cost.

Locations

Industrial developments are rarely allowed to be sited outside zones designated by the Department of the Environment. Even within these zones there are restrictions: a consultation with the local authority (LA) at an early stage can indicate whether there are likely to be problems too difficult to overcome. Naturally there is likely to be a warmer reception in areas of high unemployment and perhaps help from the LA in meeting the objections of the environmental lobby. The LA examines every project very carefully to ascertain whether any pollution is involved. Pollution can be liquid and gaseous effluents, noise, visual and social. If a public inquiry is inevitable time may be saved by employing a local consultant who is familiar with the local environment and with the attitude of the LA. The project team might be invited to provide technical information as to the different types of pollution in a formal presentation which could be subject to challenge by local objectors. The first step in the search for a suitable property would be in those strategically acceptable areas where the granting of planning permission is unlikely to be ultimately refused even though there may be several refusals before its acceptance.

The size and shape of a property on offer

Most industrial projects have an optimum layout which can give a clear indication of the ideal shape needed for the project. The optimum layout is the arrangement of buildings providing the greatest economy in the layout of structures, piping, electrical cabling etc. Departure from the ideal layout naturally increases the construction cost. To deal with this aspect the ideal layout should be drawn on a transparency, say to a scale of 1/2500 and property plans under consideration should be drawn to the same scale. The differences will then be seen. The transparency can be marked up to show access to the public highway and where connections to utilities can be made, from which costs can be estimated for use in the comparison of sites. If Ordnance Survey maps are provided by an estate/land agent the latest issue should be used and checked to ensure that all existing buildings are shown together with rights of way, public footpaths, ditches and possibly contours.

The property on offer may be too large but if the spare piece is saleable the lot may still be given consideration. The bringing of utilities to site or the provision of access to a public highway may enhance the value of this spare ground.

The project may require a reasonably level site and if so a sloping site should be regarded with caution. It is possible of course to level a site by excavation of the upper area, depositing and compacting the excavated soil on the lower area, aiming to match 'cut' and 'fill' so that no surplus soil remains to be hauled off the site. Not all soils compact easily however: loam is unsuitable except for flower beds and landscaping. Heavy clay requires very special treatment if it is not to settle appreciably under loading. Foundations for heavy loads are best founded on undisturbed soil. If excavation has to be carried out to level or terrace a site the increase in construction cost will add to the site preparation cost especially if the work is done in winter or when the soil is wet. Surplus soil resulting from such excavation may, if it is suitable, be landscaped on the perimeter of the site. The removal of soil reduces the pressure on the underlying soil and this can cause a subsequent uplift in the excavated area unless the soil removed is very shallow. Some industries can use a terraced site if a liquid feedstock is stored in tanks on the higher ground thus providing a useful pressure head for a downward flow.

The presence of an infrastructure

An infrastructure may consist of a nearby hospital, fire service, police, solid waste collection, shops, schools, doctors etc. Its absence will affect the cost of a project.

When a site is in a designated industrial zone or inner city area the location is probably already served by utilities, power, water, drains, telephones etc. There will also be public transport, possibly local workshops providing mechanical repair facilities; there may even be hotels for visitors to the new works. However, the quality of these services should be examined before any decision is confirmed. Public transport may be infrequent and unreliable in which case staff need to travel by car and this means the purchase of land for extra parking. This too may not be popular with the local people if the crowding of roads in the morning and evening leads to traffic delays. Some locations are surrounded by slums and this has been a reason for poor recruitment.

For industries using inflammable materials the presence of a fire service locally is a positive advantage. Discussion with the fire service can lead to reductions in the fire-fighting facilities needed on site. If the water main pressure or quantity is low it may be necessary to install a pressurized water ring main in locations approved by the fire service chief. Similarly a nearby hospital can reduce the extent of site first aid facilities. The Factories Act and Health and Safety legislation give guidance on this.

The presence of an infrastructure, especially schools and recreational areas, helps to attract staff to move into the locality.

Availability of skilled labour for a factory or for building construction

If the presence of skilled labour for operation is essential the Department of Trade and Industry and the local trade unions can advise on the skills available.

A shortage of labour for operating a factory could mean a delay in getting into production; this is a cost addition. If it is necessary to attract workers from a distance travel costs must somehow be paid for. Local accommodation may be available but this could be restricted to the winter months as in some seaside and country towns. The provision of permanent housing to attract skilled staff needs to be discussed with the local authorities to ensure that the area can support an influx of people and the utilities can cope. Housing tied to employment with a company can generate problems if ever there is a redundancy plan. A shortage of skills can be met by training locally unskilled or those prepared to change their skills – as for instance around old tin mining areas or coal mines – and there are government grants for this.

A shortage of building skills in the area can increase considerably the construction cost. In such trades the labour cost, normally around 50 per cent of the total cost, can increase substantially. Unless remedied the effect of a local labour shortage is to prolong the construction period and consequently the site supervision and plant hire. This kind of labour shortage can be met by engaging a large national contractor who retains his own permanent labour force and does not rely on local people for skilled men. This too has its problems: if there is insufficient local accommodation available for this temporary force a temporary construction camp will be wanted. The local authority will be concerned about this and although local shopkeepers might appreciate the extra cash in the neighbourhood, the local people in their pubs do not enjoy being crowded out. Travelling men living in a construction camp away from home expect to be able to work overtime at premium rates of pay and if this is denied (because local people work a fixed 39-hour week) the construction period may be excessive.

The condition and supporting capacity of the ground

This handbook attaches considerable importance to the need for a thorough site/soils investigation before purchase. Should the property have soil of poor supporting capacity and foundations are consequently costly, the land price though cheap may not necessarily be a bargain in the end. For instance, a high water table level will require basements and possibly foundations to be waterproofed which is an additional expense. Should the soil and water prove to be corrosive, measures to deal with this would be needed for buried concrete, steel pipes and structural steel. An inadequate understanding of the ground conditions could require remedial work to the foundations and the cost of this is likely to be out of all proportion to the original estimate. A wet site which is drained may induce ground water movement. The removal of trees which were drawing water changes the natural conditions: foundations should be established at levels which would not be affected by tree removals.

Industrial grants

The following is adapted from the Department of Trade and Industry (DTI) papers on the subject of grants with the permission of the Controller of Her Majesty's Stationery Office.

The DTI has a division 'Invest in Britain Bureau' (IBB) which can assist with all aspects of locating or relocating in the UK or expanding existing facilities. The IBB can provide information on the national and regional incentives available and can help in any contact with local government or utility services. The address is:

IBB
Department of Trade and Industry
Kingsgate House
66 – 74 Victoria Street
London SW1E 6SW   Telephone 071–215 8438

Regional selective assistance (RSA)

Some areas of the UK are in need of investment to revitalize their economies. These regions – collectively known as 'assisted areas' include those parts of England, Scotland and Wales designated as 'development areas' or 'intermediate areas'. A project grant can be offered to assist a project's capital expenditure depending on the number of jobs it is expected to create – normally in its first three years. The amount of the grant would be the minimum necessary for the project to go ahead on the basis proposed.

Eligible costs include land purchase, site preparation and buildings, plant and machinery. A manufacturing or a service industry project may qualify for RSA if it:

- has a good chance of paying its way
- will create or safeguard employment in the assisted areas
- will benefit the region and national economy
- needs assistance to go ahead.

Should a grant be needed applicants are advised not to commit themselves to a project until they have applied for assistance and received an offer. Whilst RSA is the main scheme of support for the assisted areas, another scheme, regional enterprise grants (REG), is available in development areas for small firms with fewer than 25 employees. The scheme is not automatic: projects are appraised for viability on the basis of a business plan and the firm's accounts.

Enterprise zones

There are also areas designated enterprise zones where government policy is to reinvigorate depressed areas. These zones are particularly attractive to the private sector because they offer tax advantages and streamlined development controls. The areas are in specified locations in England, Scotland, Wales and Northern Ireland. These zones are designed to run for ten years from the date of designation. They are administered by local authorities. The individual sites vary in size and character; some are based on previous wasteland while others comprise previous industrial estates with an established infrastructure. All contain land for buying or renting, some with a range of ready-built units of various sizes. Some are already landscaped.

The main benefits of locating in an enterprise zone are:

- rate-free occupation of premises
- enhanced capital allowances for taxation purposes on investment in industrial and commercial buildings
- a simplification of planning procedures.

Local authority assistance

Local authorities have general powers under which they can provide assistance to industry if this is in the local interest. This includes power to:

- advance money to acquire land
- dispose of land at below the market value.

Derelict land grant

In England in the assisted areas and derelict land clearance areas a substantial grant may be obtained. Priority is given to projects in urban, especially inner city, areas aimed at bringing derelict land back into use.

City grant

This grant aims to encourage private sector capital projects within nearly 60 priority local authorities including the areas of the Urban Development Corporation. The grant bridges the gap between the cost and the value of projects which benefit the areas allowing the investor a reasonable return on his investment. The investor gets the benefit of a city location without having to meet the abnormal costs often associated with urban areas.

Incentives in Northern Ireland

Separate and extensive powers are available to help incoming industry to operate in Northern Ireland. Companies which establish factories can receive certain standard benefits without regard to the number of jobs created.

Existing factories

In some assisted areas a number of premises – both commercial and industrial, new and previously occupied – are available for sale or lease. These may be provided for projects creating additional employment. The sizes of these premises, or 'advance factories' as they are known, range from small (50 sq. metre) workshops to large (2300 sq. metre) premises. Lease terms are determined according to local market conditions and can include an option to purchase.

There is, however, no guarantee that government factories can be made available for all inward investors wishing to locate in the assisted areas. Selective financial assistance may also be available where government factories are rented or purchased but the application for this assistance must be made before the arrangements have been settled for the factory. Any rental concession is taken into account determining the amount of selective assistance.

English Estates

The English Industrial Estates Corporation is a public corporation which works on behalf of the DTI and includes derelict land site clearance, office and workshop development and science and business parks in its operations. English Estates offers a professional property service throughout the UK and is the nation's largest industrial and commercial developer. English Estates can provide:

- factories large and small, some ready to move into
- offices – schemes in major cities fully serviced
- science parks near to research and development centres
- business parks to high specification
- warehousing, distribution and other service centres
- sites available in development areas, rural development areas and enterprise zones, all offering special assistance to people moving in.

Chapter 2

CONSTRAINTS OF THE NATURAL ENVIRONMENT ON SITE SELECTION

M.E. Griffiths

The changing face of capitalism

The countryside and development have become increasingly in conflict with recent pressures for development land in the UK and the greater public awareness of the countryside's value both for conservation and for recreational use.

There has been considerable publicity associated with large-scale developments such as power stations, coal mines, motorways and airports, and public inquiries have determined the outcome. In each case there has been a vocal and articulate public lobby on behalf of nature conservation interests under threat, often spearheaded by pressure groups such as Greenpeace or Friends of the Earth (Table 2.1).

Whereas at one time it might have been possible to push through large-scale development 'in the national interest' with little regard for the countryside, e.g. the Cow Green Reservoir in Upper Teesdale (Bines et al., 1984), this is, it is hoped, a thing of the past.

Developers and industry need to maximize profit and have their responsibilities to shareholders. In recent years more and more organizations are appreciating that their responsibilities to the countryside are also important, not least where this becomes financially pragmatic – optimizing rather than maximizing profit.

Public relations are all-important where this influences the likelihood of

Table 2.1 *Development proposals modified due to nature conservation concerns*

Development	Nature conservation concern
M40 (Oxfordshire)	Otmoor ancient pastures
Vale of Belvoir coal mine	Saxelby Hanger woodland
Midline oil pipeline	Oxton Ditch marsh warblers
Sizewell 'B' road access	Wetland wildlife
Third London airport	Foulness Brent geese

future acceptance of development proposals and the sale of products. The press and TV are full of advertisements by oil companies, large corporations and others proclaiming their responsible attitude towards the countryside.

Despite greater responsibility from some quarters legislation has been necessary to protect the countryside from the less responsible. Voluntary codes are insufficient guarantees in a free market economy. Hence the various statutory regulations from the UK and the EEC to provide some measure of control over the 'cowboy developer'. The only exception seems to be agricultural development where the consequences of the at-present ineffective statutory controls are a cause for concern (see Green, 1984).

Planners need to take into account the statutory regulations, as well as compare the likely advantages of an area's development with the disadvantages, such as the impact on sensitive sites of nature conservation interest.

A small developer without the financial muscle or knowhow of the multinationals may be tempted to take short cuts where site selection involves an ecological consideration. This may result in infringement of the law and financial penalties.

Main ecological concerns for developers

Ecologists and conservationists are typified in the eyes of many as the 'butterfly brigade', who stand in the way of progress because of some butterfly or other animal or plant likely to be destroyed by some essential development.

Such objections may appear trivial, but it is true that in some cases a rare species may be of some concern, and in most cases these species are indicators of an unusual habitat in need of preservation nationally.

Rare species sometimes turn up unexpectedly after planning permission is sought, not just because of the cussedness of interest groups, but often because habitats under threat are not investigated thoroughly by the experts until the threat materializes. This is due to lack of resources of the conservation organizations and the need to concentrate these scarce resources where most needed.

There are two broad aspects of the countryside most under threat from development that are the concern of the general public and conservationists:

- *the general countryside* with its rural landscape and typical countryside features of woodland, hedgerows, fields, ponds, rivers, coastland etc. This has aesthetic visual features, as well as intrinsic value in terms of recreational amenity and nature conservation interest such as the butterflies, rabbits, frogs and birds that typify our natural environment.
- *specific sites* of special scientific interest (SSSI) including rare habitats and individual rare species or assemblages of plants and animals.

The former are the professional concern of landscape architects, and our local authority representatives, with the statutory body being the Countryside Commission, as well as voluntary organizations such as the Council for the Preservation of Rural England.

The SSSI are the particular professional concern of conservationists and the statutory body, the Nature Conservancy Council (NCC), as well as voluntary bodies such as the county nature conservation trusts.

The general countryside

The value of general countryside features and the amount of concern to be expected from interested parties is related to how natural these features are, their species and habitat rarity, the diversity of fauna and flora, how extensive the area is, as well as whether or not they occur in the 'green belt'. In effect there are few if any natural features of nature conservation interest remaining in the UK, and any such would have special protection, but examples of *semi-natural* features in need of conservation and which should be taken into account by developers are given below (see also Rackham, 1986):

- deciduous (or natural forest) woodland, especially ancient woodland
- ancient hedgerows, characterized by a large variety of woody species
- unimproved grassland with little if any application of fertilizers or agricultural pesticides, characterized by a high species diversity of plants and invertebrates
- any natural or semi-natural wetland area – marshes, bogs, ponds, dykes, rivers and streams
- field margins and roadside verges
- heathland and moorland
- estuarine or marine intertidal habitats
- offshore marine environment.

Sites of special scientific interest

Throughout the UK there are about 6000 well defined sites of differing size covering 8 per cent of the land surface. These are sites of special scientific interest (SSSIs) and are exceptional areas of special interest by reason of their flora, fauna, geological or physiographic features and include most national nature reserves. Under the Wildlife and Countryside Act 1981 they are designated by, and their protection is the responsibility of, the Nature Conservancy Council (see Ratcliffe, 1977).

SSSIs, national parks and areas of outstanding natural beauty (AONBs) are the main specific areas where development will be restricted by the planning authorities on the grounds of the nature conservation interest.

Before giving planning permission for any development affecting an SSSI the local planning authority must first consult the NCC. The NCC have three months to consider an application and to consult with the developer how best to further the nature conservation interests of the site if permission for development is not to be opposed.

Some proposed developments in national nature reserves will be forwarded first by planning authorities to the NCC and the Countryside Commission for their consideration.

Some proposed developments in AONBs will be forwarded first by planning authorities to the Countryside Commission for their consideration.

The NCC representative will probably need to make an on-site inspection with the developer to help in the decision. The NCC will need to be convinced that there is no alternative to the involvement of an SSSI in a proposed development, and that all proper measures are taken to prevent or reduce to a minimum ecological damage.

Under current legislation the NCC will pass on to the developer information he requires concerning the designation of an area as an SSSI.

In most areas of the UK there are second-tier sites of nature conservation interest (SNCI or SINC) which are non-statutory and either designated by the county council or the local, independent, Nature Conservation Trust. There are many more of these sites than SSSIs, and they are regarded by the NCC as having less nature conservation significance than an SSSI, although subject to review. Increasingly these sites are being taken into account by local planning authorities when considering development proposals, and they may in future be brought within the statutory system (Andrews and Box, 1988).

Effects of different types of development on the natural environment

The development of greenfield sites by housing and industrial developers may affect any of the types of countryside mentioned above. Some of the effects could be the direct destruction of habitat or wildlife, while other effects may be incidental and difficult to quantify.

Direct effects include the removal of trees (some protected under a tree preservation order – TPO), woodland, hedgerows, and the drainage or destruction of wetland habitats.

Incidental effects include pollution from industry, and other nuisance such as dumping and vandalism associated with the urbanization of the countryside.

Some leisure activities, often added by a developer as a 'sweetener' to attract local support, may conflict with nature conservation interests. Water sports, in particular sail-boarding and water skiing, are not compatible with waterfowl in wetlands (Tanner, 1979).

Different types of industry, such as wood pulp, printing and dyeing, tanneries and chemical plants, have specific pollution problems associated with their particular processes. The effects may be insidious and difficult to assess. The National Rivers Authority (NRA) has a statutory duty to assess likely pollution, largely for consequences on human health as well as effects on the general ecology, and to advise industry on consent criteria. Future consent criteria are likely to be more stringent to comply with EEC regulations (Johnson, 1983).

There have been a number of ecological problems resulting from development, usually industrial, that caused financial costs or embarrassment to the developer such as those in Table 2.1. Many of these costs could have been avoided by better forward planning to foresee and mitigate these ecological effects. Assessment of the natural environment in the neighbourhood of a proposed development should be regarded by a developer as financially prudent as well as environmentally responsible.

Environmental impact assessment

An environmental impact assessment (EIA) is a document produced by a developer, in a structured, standardized format for defining planning proposals and their likely impact on the environment. This informs planners and other interested or affected parties, and allows for the proper consideration of a proposal. The technique was developed in North America where EIAs have been well established over many years (e.g. Heer and Haggerty, 1977).

Large developments such as power stations, pipelines and oil refineries etc. have far-reaching implications for the ecology of an area which may involve effects on a number of natural communities. Such developments require detailed study of the local ecology and the likely impact. Under recent legislation (Town and Country Planning Regulations 1988) a detailed environmental impact assessment (EIA) and possibly a public inquiry are required, at the discretion of the Secretary of State, before planning permission is granted.

At the discretion of the local planning authority an EIA can be requested for other developments, especially where sited in sensitive areas.

An EIA is normally produced for a developer by independent experts under the required topics. The likely impact on nature conservation interests is one area that must be covered.

The EIA will include the details of the proposed development, as well as any processes involved and details of the sensitive sites in the area likely to be affected. Details of sites of nature conservation interest should be included with adequate survey work undertaken to indicate the biological characteristics of the sites. Anticipated impact of the development should be assessed and alternative sites considered. Any mitigation of impact and compensatory work proposed should be noted.

An EIA should be regarded by a large developer as a continuous process, not merely a means to gaining planning consent. This is especially true in the case of effluent discharge, where continuous monitoring is essential to confirm the anticipated impact on the natural communities and consequences for health.

The costs of an adequate EIA can be high where prior survey work is necessary, and care should be taken to avoid data overkill which can be counterproductive. There are many published examples of the type of survey that may be necessary (e.g. Roberts and Roberts, 1984 and Munn, 1979).

Kent – a county with nature conservation on the defensive

Kent has considerable development both existing and proposed, associated with its position in the southeast, closest to continental Europe. One-third of all current planning applications in England are in Kent (Everett and Prytherch, 1990 p. 87), with such major developments underway as the Channel tunnel, the M20 extension, and proposed developments including the rail link and the Medway–Swale reclamation.

Many of these developments have an impact on nature conservation interests in a county rich in wildlife. The Kent Countryside Plan (1983) sets out policies and proposals regarding development, and other uses of land, and defines the various areas of special significance for countryside conservation, identified in the Kent Structure Plan (1980) and illustrated in Figure 2.1.

In common with similar planning strategies in many other counties, priority conservation areas are protected from development by the local planning authority through the structure plan:

- Special landscape areas (SLA) have long-term protection giving priority to their scenic value over other planning considerations.
- Areas of high nature conservation value (AHNCV) are important areas

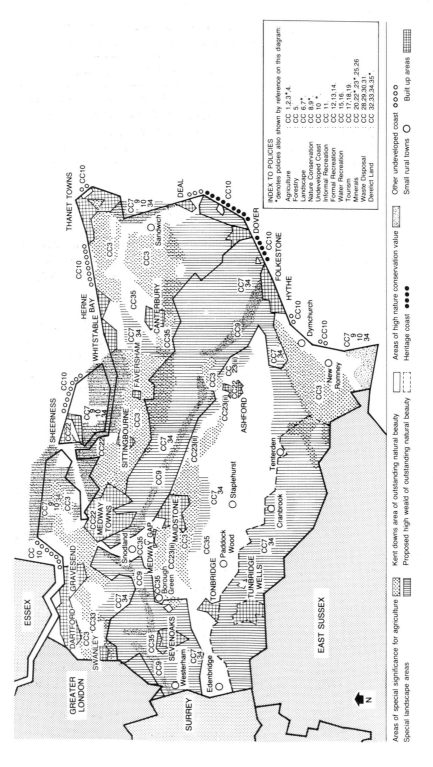

Figure 2.1 *Kent Structure Plan – countryside and coast.*
Reproduced with permission from Kent County Council Planning Department.

Table 2.2 *Examples where forward planning allowing for nature conservation interests may have reduced development costs in Kent*

Development	Nature conservation interest
Channel tunnel – tunnel entry	Holywell Escarpment – botanical
Channel tunnel – spoil disposal	Dungeness Gravel Pits – birds
M20 Maidstone bypass	Greater Broomrape site
Ramsgate Harbour access road	Rare algae on Pegwell Cliff

where the policy does not permit development harmful to the maintenance of scarce and potentially vulnerable wildlife habitats.

● Undeveloped coasts are protected from urban or industrial development if it materially detracts from the unspoilt scenic quality or scientific value of the undeveloped coastline or in the adjoining countryside.

Recent developments in Kent have been modified at the planning stage at considerable cost to the developer due to concerns over nature conservation interests at risk (Table 2.2). In some cases the planning application has failed due, in part at least, to such concerns. With better forward planning by the developer such costs, including in some cases a costly public inquiry, would have been avoided.

Mitigation of impact on nature conservation interests

Where planned developments impinge unavoidably on areas of nature conservation interest successful applications should include *mitigation* and *compensation*.

Mitigation includes reducing impact by careful on-the-spot control of a development, e.g. not felling trees but incorporating them sensitively in landscaping around a site; replacing turf containing rare plant species after laying a pipeline; minimizing damage to a site through reducing the working area; liaison with nature conservation bodies over methodology and monitoring.

Compensation is best effected through creative conservation projects such as the inclusion of a proposal for a nature reserve in the planning proposal.

There are however few, if any, examples of sites of nature conservation interest successfully recreated once destroyed (see Buckley, 1989), and conservationists are understandably sceptical of any such plans in a development proposal.

Kent examples of mitigation in development planning are best illustrated by the following aspects of the Channel tunnel work:

- Re-established habitat, e.g. Biggins Wood – moved topsoil and seed stock in an attempt to re-establish wood.
- Re-alignment of route, e.g. Holywell Coombe – alignment of tunnel to avoid geological and archaeological deposits.
- Monitoring programmes:
  - changes in soil structure
  - escarpment at terminal
  - effects on Dover cliffs
  - streams for water quality
  - Shakespeare Cliff for marine and plant interest.
- Financial input: White Cliffs Countryside Project.

Cost-effective site selection

It is becoming increasingly clear that cost-effective site selection means responsible site selection. Public opinion and legislation between them will ensure that if certain rules are ignored by developers, in relation to the nature conservation interest of a proposed development site, this will result in considerable cost. It is suggested that the following steps should be taken:

1. Before writing and submitting the planning application establish the likely concerns of the planning authority regarding the nature conservation interests of the locality in addition to any local authority structure plan.
2. Check especially that there are no SSSIs or NNRs in the region of the proposed development, and that the area is not a national park or an area of outstanding natural beauty (AONB).
3. Check for areas of local nature conservation interest (e.g. SNCI or SINC) in the area and assess their sensitivity to the proposed development.
4. Be open and clear about possible emissions or effluents from industrial plants to the NRA and assess the likely impact on the ecology before applying for planning permission.
5. Keep to a minimum any effect on the general countryside such as trees, woodland, hedgerows, unimproved grassland, wetland. Assess this beforehand with expert assistance.
6. Where some ecological effect on an SSSI seems unavoidable, early consultation with the NCC is essential.
7. Where some ecological effect on the general countryside seems unavoidable, before the planning application stage seek expert advice for keeping effects to a minimum and consider the possibility of compensatory ecological proposals.
8. When in doubt have an EIA professionally prepared at an early stage, even if this is not requested by the local planning authority. Inform the LPA of this intention and discuss with them their requirements.

References

Andrews, J. and Box, J. (1988), '*SINC's go swimmingly'*. *Urban Wildlife*, June, pp.32–33.

Bines, T.J. et al. (1984), 'A retrospective view of Environmental Impact on Upper Teesdale of the Cow Green Reservoir' in Roberts, R.D. and Roberts T.M. (eds), *Planning and Ecology*, Chapman and Hall, London.

Buckley, G.P. (ed.) (1989), *Biological Habitat Reconstruction*, Bell Haven Press, London.

Countryside Review Committee (1976), *The Countryside – problems and policies*, HMSO, London.

European Commission (1978), *Methods of Environmental Impact Assessment for major projects and physical plans (ENV/36/78)* Brussels.

Everett, M. and Prytherch, R. (1990), 'News and Comment – Developments in Kent' *British Birds*, vol. 83, no. 2, February, p.87.

Green, B.H. (1984) 'Planning a New Countryside'. In Roberts R.D. and Roberts T.M. (eds), *Planning and Ecology*, Chapman and Hall, London and New York.

Heer, J.E. and Haggerty, D.J. (1977), *Environmental Assessments and Statements*, Van Nostrand Reinhold, New York.

Johnson, P.J. (1983), *The Pollution Control Policy of The European Communities*. Graham and Trotman, London.

Kent Countryside Local Plan. Written Statement. Kent County Council, Planning Department. 1983.

Kent Structure Plan. Kent County Council, Planning Department. 1980.

Munn, R.E. (ed.) (1979), *Environmental Impact Assessment: Principles and Procedures*, John Wiley and Sons, London.

Nature Conservation Sites in Kent. Kent County Council. 1988.

Rackham, O. (1986), *The History of The Countryside*. Dent, London and Melbourne.

Ramsgate Harbour Access Road Public Inquiry: Construction of New Single Carriageway Harbour Access Road. Application by Kent County Council. D.O.E. 17 June 1988. Charles House, London.

Ratcliffe, D.A. (1977), *A Nature Conservation Review*. 2 vols. Cambridge University Press. Cambridge.

Roberts, R.D. and Roberts, T.M. (eds) (1984), *Planning and Ecology*. Chapman and Hall. London and New York.

Stevens Committee (1976), *Planning Control over Mineral Working*, HMSO, London.

Tanner, M.F. (1979), 'Review of disturbance to wintering wildfowl'. *Wildfowl, reservoirs and recreation*. Research Report No. 5, Water Space Amenity Commission.

Town and Country Planning (*Assessment of Environmental Effects*) Regulations, 1988.

Vale of Belvoir Coalfield Inquiry (The North East Leicestershire prospect) Inquiry Report. HMSO, London, 1980.

Wildlife and Countryside Act (1981) Amended 1984. HMSO, London, 1984.

Wildlife and Countryside Act (1981): section 33. *Code of guidance for Sites of Special Scientific Interest*. HMSO, London, 1981.

Chapter 3

SITE SELECTION FOR AN INDUSTRIAL DEVELOPMENT

R.A. Robinson

Finding a suitable site

Finding a site suitable for development is becoming increasingly difficult and there is considerable competition for good sites. If a development scheme is to be successful the price must be competitive and market conditions correctly evaluated: errors can be costly.

Before setting out to purchase a site a developer should prepare a policy regarding:

1. The maximum financial investment available
2. The geographical areas under consideration
3. The source of funding for the scheme.

As soon as this has been agreed by all interested parties an approach can be made to land agents. Land agents are accustomed to sorting out serious clients from the others and will soon know if their time is being wasted.

The amount of investment

The amount of investment proposed for a development naturally depends on the developer's own policies, but the proposed location for the operation can also influence the amount available. For instance a twenty million pound project in Slough could be considered reasonable for the locality and for an institutional funding but it would be excessive for say, Amersham. Whether it would be a good investment, depends on the price of a property and 'what the market will bear'. Simply because there may be a demand for such sites does not necessarily mean they will be successful ventures. If there are doubts about this, professional advice should be sought.

Suitable locations for a development

Locations considered suitable for a development may be a matter of company policy or there may be a simple preference for sites which are within easy travel of the company's office. The site itself should be able to have the following features:

For an offices development
1. Good access to road and rail services
2. Be near to other offices

Consideration should also be given to:

1. The size of office buildings already existing or due to be built and
2. The amount of vacant office space in the locality.

For an industrial development
1. Access to a motorway or other trunk road system
2. Its location in relation to other industrial sites
3. The amount of vacant space in the area and the demand for this.

The size of other industrial properties in the area is also relevant.

For a prime shopping area
1. The proximity to the main shopping area is of importance as is its position to the movement of shoppers by pedestrian crossings or the approaches to car parks etc.
2. The amount of vacant space in the area under consideration and whether rents and rates increases are affecting the shops.

For a residential scheme
1. The locality – views, access, public transport, proximity to shops
2. Type of housing in the vicinity
3. The number of other developments and amenities being built.

The most important factor in valuation of a site is its position. As an example, the value of a shop on the 'better' side of a street can be worth double or even more than a shop on the less desirable side.

The source of funding for the scheme

The source and amount of finance available must be confirmed before any dealings with a land agent begin. The property market is disturbed if it is known that an offer for a property has been made and accepted, only to find that the deal cannot be completed because the finance is not available.

If the developer does not have his own funds there are various ways of raising capital as follows:

1. A bank loan
   A loan may be offered by a clearing or merchant bank for up to two thirds of the total development cost. Normal interest and commitment fees are charged; security for the loan will have to be agreed.
2. Joint venture
   A Joint Venture is a shared risk by a financial organization putting up the cash and the developer managing and directing the project. When the project is complete profits or losses are shared equally.
3. Limited recourse finance
   Under this arrangement a financier puts up say 80 per cent of the total capital needed and the developer puts in his stake of 20 per cent. When the project is complete profits are divided 20 per cent to the financier and 80 per cent to the developer. If there are losses the financier bears any loss greater than the developer's original stake.
4. Finance by the contractor building the project
   The developer responsible for the purchase of the site selects a contractor willing to finance the construction work. When the development is complete and sold there is a settlement, profits and losses are sorted out using a predetermined arrangement.
5. Prefunding
   The project is sold in advance to a funding institution for an agreed sum. During the construction the institution provides funds to pay costs up to the agreed sum, interest charges are included in this amount.

Other matters

Apart from financial matters the following should be considered:

1. Can the project be easily handled by the developer; for example, is the site convenient to the developer's office?
2. Is there any possibility that Planning Permission might be refused?
3. Has the proposal been discussed with the Local Authority?
4. Is the property worth the price being asked?
5. Will the site be easy to sell when complete in, say, a year's time?
6. Are the ground conditions satisfactory?

7.   Have there been problems on adjacent sites?

Most developers know what is going on in their locality and the 'other matters' above present no problem.

Finding the site

People selling land today (1990) are more aware of the value of land than formerly. Most land owners employ a professional land agent to sell their property and since agents normally aim to get the best price there are few bargains. The easiest and quickest way to locate a suitable site especially in an area unknown to the prospective purchaser is to employ a land agent. These agents have several ways of finding sites for consideration including:

1.   Details of land for sale are circulated among agents
2.   Agents may have clients of their own with land for sale
3.   Trade journals and local newspapers carry advertisements
4.   'For sale' notices may be put up on sites for sale
5.   Local Authorities may have or know of land for sale
6.   Agents may know land owners who may be persuaded to sell land.

The intending purchaser should invite his agent to prepare a special report on suitable properties. This report should deal with the following:

1.   The location of the site relative to local towns and villages
2.   A description of surrounding area
3.   Road, rail or waterway access, presence of utilities
4.   The present and past usage of the site and its present condition
5.   Details of similar developments to the one now proposed
6.   Whether there is any likelihood of Planning Permission being refused
7.   The agent's own valuation of the land and details of the prices paid on adjacent sites.

If possible this report should be accompanied by an Ordnance Survey map on which the proposed development has been superimposed.

This report could then be used by the developer in any submission he has to make to his senior management to aid the decision on whether to proceed with the land purchase.

An agent should not be considered as a specialist in every discipline connected with land and it may be advisable to have professional advice on:

1.   Whether a soils investigation is necessary
2.   If so, whether the ground conditions are likely to increase the cost of construction

3. Whether there could be any boundary problems
4. Whether a site survey should be made if there are obstructions on the site.

Boundaries

The site boundaries should be examined on site to see whether they conform with the property deeds and Land Registry plans. Any discrepancies will need to be clarified and this is best done by a solicitor. The reason for having a site survey is that solicitors do not always visit a site and a survey by professional surveyors enables discrepancies to become apparent. The ownership of boundary markers should be determined. Among the disputes following land purchase the majority seem to be concerned with boundaries. Disputes after purchase can affect the value of an investment.

Planning permission

Unless there is a certainty of obtaining Planning Permission it can be waste of time to consider any site for development; however many refusals can be changed to acceptances if the Local Authority's amendments are introduced. Where there are problems and doubts a Planning consultant can earn his fee if he gets matters sorted out prior to purchase. In this respect the following is adviseable, unless already investigated by the agent:

1. An inspection of the Local Authority local and structural plans to verify their policies regarding the proposed development.
2. An examination of the Planning register to ascertain whether consents have been granted for near or similar developments.
3. A visit to the surrounding properties to see which other developments have been undertaken.
4. Ask the Local Authority whether the existing use of the site could affect the grant of Planning Permission.

If the site is within a conservation or green belt area or contains a building or feature of archaeological interest (i.e. listed) advice from professionals is essential. Sites in green belt areas are rarely offered as development sites and should be considered only if Planning Permission is guaranteed.

Section 52 agreements

If an application for Planning Permission is refused and it is a borderline case the Local Authority may be prepared to regard the application as acceptable if the developer is willing to provide an amenity or local improvement. For instance the construction of a public footpath or the improvement of a river bank might tip the balance. This is known as a Section 52 Agreement. There is no subsequent appeal once agreement has been reached.

The value of a site

The value of a site varies in accordance with the use made of it although land agents can assess its value by comparison with prices obtained from the sale of similar plots in the same locality. For a development, the value can be assessed by the 'Residual Valuation' method. This is done by first assuming that the development is complete and calculating what its revenue would total at the end of its payback period. From this sum a deduction is made for the total cost of construction including bank interest and professional fees. The amount remaining is the value of the land. The following examples show how the calculation is done.

Example of a Residual Valuation

A development comprises a group of offices and an industrial building both with car parking spaces.

		£
Assume the office rents as		
16 000 ft^2 @ £25 per ft^2 per annum	=	400 000
The yield on this is 6.5% p.a.		
Revenue is $\frac{100}{6.5} \times 400\,000$	=	6 153 800
Less stamp duty, solicitors fees and agents fees all at 2½%	=	153 800
Net realization	=	6 000 000
Assume industrial building rents as		
10 800 ft^2 @ £7 per ft^2 per annum	=	75 600
The yield on this is taken at 8.0 % p.a.		
Revenue is $\frac{100}{8} \times 75\,600$	=	945 000
Less 2½% as above	=	23 625
		921 375
Total being the Net Realization Values		6 921 375
say		£6 921 500

To estimate the construction costs for the above:

Assume site preparation	=	20 000	
Assume erection costs			
Offices say 20 000 ft^2 @ £80 per ft^2	=	1 600 000	
Industrial say 12 000 ft^2 @ £32 per ft^2	=	384 000	
Roads and services allow	=	30 000	
subtotal	(i)		2 014 000

Fees, Engineer 2½–3%, Architect 5½–6%
Surveyor 2–2½% total 12½% (ii) 251 750
Other costs to be added

Fees to agents for letting say one in London, one local		
15% of (400 000 plus 75 600)	=	71 340
Fees to agents for the sale		
1.5% of 6 920 000	=	103 800
Legal expenses ½% of 6 920 000	=	34 600
Building Regulations and Planning		
Permission fees	=	10 000
Contingency, miscellaneous agents charges		
not included above	=	65 000
		284 740

Bank loan interest charges: assume 2 years to complete the site, loan accrues from zero to (£20 000 plus 2 014 000 plus 251 750) i.e. £2 285 750 @ 16% p.a. (average 8%)	=	182 860
Assume property unlet for 6 months interest ½ × 16% [(i) plus (ii) above plus 182 860] i.e. ½ × 16% of £2 468 560	=	197 500
Profit, say 15% of £6 920 000	=	1 038 000
	=	3 988 850
Total Estimated Construction Costs say	=	£3 990 000

Summary Residual Valuation for the Above

Net realization value as shown	=	6 921 500
Estimated construction costs say	=	3 990 000
difference		2 931 500

This represents the cost of the property,

plus its interest charges and all
associated fees

Interest for 2 years plus a half year unlet	=	585 000

Property and associated purchasing fees	=	2 345 000

Purchasing fees
1% stamp duty, ½% solicitor, 1% agents
acquisition fees

total 2½%	=	58 600

Difference being the *Residual Valuation*	=	2 286 400
say	=	£2 300 000

Another Example of Residual Valuation for a Residential Scheme

Assume

20 × 3bed houses			
@ £100 000 each	=	2 000 000	
10 × 2bed houses			
@ £90 000	=	900 000	
10 × 2bed houses			
@ £100 000 (better views)	=	1 000 000	
10 × 1bed flats			
@ £78 000	=	780 000	
2 × 1bed flats			
@ £85 000 (roof-tops)	=	170 000	
52 dwellings assumed value when complete	=		4 850 000

Estimate of cost for the above			
Site preparation	=	20 000	
Roads and sewers	=	100 000	
Erection of houses and flats estimated	=	2 534 000	
Professional fees (architect £1000			
engineer £500)			
52 × £1 500	=	78 000	
subtotal			2 732 000

Other costs to be added			
Fees to agents for letting 2% × £4 850 000	=	97 000	
Legal expenses ½% × £4 850 000	=	24 250	
Marketing costs and Show House say	=	16 000	
National House Builders certificates			
52 × £400	=	20 800	
Planning Permission and Building			
Regulation fees say	=	10 000	
Contingency allow	=	30 000	

Profit 15% × £4 850 000   =   727 500
Interest ½ year @ 16% × £2 732 000   =   218 560

                                    subtotal   1 144 110

Total Estimated Construction Costs   3 876 110

Summary Residual Valuation for the Residential Scheme

Net realization value as shown   4 850 000
Estimated Construction Costs   3 876 110

                          difference   973 890
Deduct interest charges   155 800
Purchasing fees @ 2½%
(973 850–155 800)   20 450

                                                                           176 250

                                                                                         797 640
                                    say   £   800 000
                                    This is the Residual Valuation

The prices for the dwellings in the above example may be either current prices or enhanced for the future, i.e. when the project is complete.

Freehold or leasehold sites

If investors are needed to finance a development their usual preference is freehold rather than leasehold.

Purchasing a property

The method of purchasing a site is usually stipulated by the seller. If he wants a 'Sale by tender' the 'best once and for all' price is offered. 'Sale by auction' allows a prospective bidder to increase his offer to his own limit. Sale 'by private treaty' means that the seller can negotiate privately.

Legal matters

Once an offer has been accepted the next step is to ask a solicitor to deal with the transaction and to prepare a contract. A purchase by 'tender' or 'auction' is always 'subject to contract'. The terms of the contract should include:

1.   The price to be paid and when

2. A description of the property in detail
3. The completion date for the transaction
4. The terms and conditions as agreed, for instance 'subject to obtaining Planning Permission'.

Before presenting a contract for signature the solicitor will also deal with:

1. Deducing, for instance, tracing and verifying the title to the property
2. Ensuring that conditions will be met for example, the obtaining of Planning Permission
3. Ensuring that there are no problems with the boundaries
4. Ensuring that there are no restrictive covenants, tenancies, rights of way or similar which might impede the sale
5. Ensuring that there are no ambiguities in the contract and that the agreed terms are understood by both purchaser and seller.

As soon as the solicitor is satisfied that the contract is in order he should present it for signature. The purchaser should then study the documents and anything not absolutely clear should be discussed with the solicitor. After signature the seller may ask for a deposit, possibly ten per cent of the price. The purchaser is recommended to request that the deposit be held by the solicitor as 'stakeholder' rather than giving it directly to the seller.

Completion of purchase

From the moment that contracts are exchanged the purchaser is liable for the insurance of the property. The interval between 'exchange of contracts' and 'completion' is normally 28 days though for commercial properties it may be less. During this period application for Planning Permission should be progressed, this could save time and interest on any loan.

Vacant possession

If the agreement is to provide vacant possession on completion of the purchase it is not recommended to accept the seller's promise to give vacant possession. Completion monies should only be handed over if the agreed conditions are fully met.

Summary of important matters

● Before seeking a plot, the proposed scheme should ideally be defined with a layout

- The source and amount of funding should be settled
- The areas considered suitable to locate the development should be stated together with requirements for access, utilities, level surface etc.
- If a valuation of the site is required this should be prepared at current prices, with due recognition of location and position
- If an inspection or site investigation is needed it should be carried out by a professional
- It is better to ask too many questions than to find out later that something has been missed
- Many profits have been made on property but there have also been many losses·
- Investors in recent times (1990) who relied on inflation of property prices have in some cases made heavy losses
- The purchasing of land and property calls for specialist knowledge.

Chapter 4

ACCESS AND UTILITIES

Dan Lampert

Sites for development which are remote from utilities (power, water, drains) are normally cheaper to buy or rent than those provided with utilities. Value for money, however, can only be determined after a comparison of cost studies for bringing utilities to site together with all other incidental expenses.

Electricity for power

The presence of high voltage overhead power cables requires the installation of transformer and switch houses to provide for a low voltage source for distribution within a site. Unless the quantity of power needed on site is exceptionally high the cost of this is likely to be charged to or shared with the consumer. Today (1990) there is discussion of the electricity industry being privatized. If it is, the price of electricity will vary throughout the UK. Large users can expect to be able to negotiate power prices before settling on any location. The information the power company would need is:

- the maximum daily power demand and the power factor
- whether the demand is during the day, night or shiftwork
- whether the load would fluctuate much and if so the peak load
- what the power would be used for, e.g. rotating equipment, welding, heating, air conditioning etc.
- whether the demand can tolerate an interruption in supply.

After privatization is introduced the supply of electricity will be non-franchised. Companies which generate their own power may be able to offer some for sale.

Interruptions in supply of power

There are industries which cannot tolerate interruptions in power supply, e.g. process plants in the oil industry. When this happens emergency standby supplies are brought immediately into action. Standby generating equipment is operated by steam (if there is a steam-producing facility) or by diesel, petrol or batteries. Interruptions have been caused by overloading, storms, snow and industrial action. The frequency of interruptions varies throughout the UK and information on this may be obtained from the Electricity Council, Millbank, London SW1.

Water

Water supply

If a project demands high consumption of water, consultation with the local water authority is advisable before deciding on a location. In 1989 shortages in some areas lasted several weeks. Water authorities are now laying pipelines around the UK to ease the problem. Should the demand for water be modest a standby service can be provided by having an on-site storage tank sufficient in capacity to cater for a short interruption in supplies. Construction of an elevated tank to provide pressure for distribution around the site should be included in costs. Water treatment plant is wanted for some hard waters.

Surface water drainage

The collection of surface water from paved areas is normally through gullies into drainpipes which discharge into ditches or drains. Should this water become contaminated it would have to go through some form of treatment before discharge from site.

If the site needs to be drained and discharged into a water course (other than a public sewer) the local water authority must be consulted. Water from boreholes must be reasonably free from mud, silt or offensive matter before discharge. Most water authorities have a betterment policy with their rivers: if the river is say ten parts per million polluted, water drawn can only be returned to the river with five parts per million pollution.

Artesian wells

The abstraction of underground or subterranean water from artesian wells requires a licence from the water authority if the water will be used as part of a continuous operation. Supplies can be controlled by the authority.

Fire hydrants

For some industries the local fire authority can ask for fire hydrants to be installed on site. Consultation with this authority is needed to agree convenient places for installation. If the authority asks for water mains in the site to be oversized in order to meet their fire-fighting requirements they may contribute to the cost of the oversizing. In such cases site owners should clarify with the fire authority who is responsible for the maintenance of the hydrants.

Natural gas

The schedule of prices for the supply of natural gas in commercial quantities depends on the quantity to be consumed and whether the supply may be interrupted by the gas company. Contracts are therefore 'firm' or 'interruptible' supply. Interruptions can occur in winter or spring or if there is an exceptionally cold spell. If the factory/installation cannot permit an interruption, emergency supplies must be provided to come into effect immediately. This is done by having fuel-oil burners adjacent to the gas burners in any furnace, the fuel-oil system coming into operation if there is a failure in the gas supply. The amount of fuel-oil to be stored for such an emergency would depend on the period of interruption of the gas supply and the period required for replenishment of the fuel-oil supplies. Gas companies can cut supplies at four hours' notice although the total length of interruptions in any contract year can be agreed in advance. The tariff for an 'interruptible' supply of gas is of course cheaper than for a 'firm' supply.

British Gas is usually prepared to negotiate prices with prospective major users and would need to know:

- the gas-using equipment to be installed
- the pattern of the use of gas
- the peak consumption in therms
- the estimated annual consumption
- the minimum pressures needed.

British Gas offer a technical consultancy service to assist in installing equipment. Any work must be done by British Gas or one of its approved contractors and the consumer may have to share in the cost.

Telephones

There are few problems with the installation of telephones other than having to wait for a connection. British Telecom can normally advise on the time needed to connect a subscriber and this could include any time needed to increase the capacity of the local telephone exchange centre if necessary. If a telephone cable has to be brought to site British Telecom reserve the right to ask for a contribution towards the cost.

Access

Freight facilities grant scheme

Goods and materials usually arrive or leave the site on road vehicles. The main exceptions are coal, ores, quarry material and the like. The movement of such freight by rail or inland waterway especially between one private siding or wharf and another has far less impact on the environment than if it were moved by road. The capital cost of building sidings and wharves, however, can make the provision of these facilities uneconomic when compared with road transport.

The Department of Transport, in recognition of the environmental benefits obtained from the movement of freight by rail or inland waterway awards grants towards the capital cost of new or modernized facilities such as private sidings or wharves. Applicants must demonstrate that their proposed facilities will result in a worthwhile reduction of lorry traffic from unsuitable roads and could not be commercially considered without grant. The extent of the grant could be up to 50 per cent of the costs provided the Department of Transport criteria are met.

The above information on freight facilities grants and what follows has been extracted from the Department of Transport's current (1990) guidance on these grants and has been reproduced with their kind permission.

The amount of any grant has to be justified by the environmental benefits and the financial case. In addition to the grant there is the possibility of obtaining capital tax allowances on the net expenditure after receipt of grant. The grant does not apply however if it is in the applicant's commercial interest to use rail or inland waterway or there is no practical road alternative.

The environmental benefits would take account of:

- the number and frequency of road movements which would be avoided during the life of the project
- the size and type of the road vehicles which would have been used
- the road routes over which the road vehicles would have to travel
- the comments of local authorities on the effect of the project on their areas

In awarding grants the Department of Transport expects the facilities to provide long-term benefits (usually ten years although shorter periods can be negotiated). A minimum qualifying period is included in the conditions attached to the grant but if railway wagons or cargo-carrying vessels are involved this period is ten years. The traffic in question would have to use the facilities for the minimum period specified. Cost figures demonstrating that the investment would not be commercially justified without grant would have to be supplied. Any grant requested would be towards the initial expenditure on capital items and these should normally have an anticipated life at least as long as the qualifying life of the project.

The following expenditure can be considered for grant:

- purchase of land, the price being subject to approval
- environmental damage prevention, e.g. reduction of dust
- maintenance of any rights of way
- design costs
- refurbishing costs
- cost of rail-track and signalling
- material handling equipment, e.g. cranes, conveyors etc.
- installation of utilities
- access ways to loading/unloading points
- storage and administrative buildings
- shunting locomotives and rolling stock

For an inland waterway facility the following could be considered for grant:

- terminals for loading and unloading of freight
- equipment needed for the above, e.g. wharves, jetties, quays, moorings, basins and turning pools, flood gates and flood locks, associated earthworks, towpaths, towpath bridges, signalling and cabling equipment.

Improvement of existing facilities could also qualify for grant if this would avoid additional traffic on roads.

The grant is intended to tip the financial balance in favour of rail or inland waterway. The letting of contracts or commencing work in advance of a decision to award grant could prejudice the award as this could imply that the project would go ahead in any case. The grant would not usually be paid in such circumstances. Similarly a grant would not be paid if there were a restriction in obtaining planning permission, i.e. permission being granted conditional on the use of rail. British Rail or the navigation authority would of course have to approve the facilities and be prepared to carry the traffic. Facilities unlikely to attract grant are those not required specifically for the handling of freight by rail or inland waterway, e.g. buildings where items are made or sold. Other costs excluded from the grant would be establishment charges and overheads during the design and construction of the facilities and similar unrelated expenses.

Application for a grant for rail/waterway facilities should be accompanied by details of the proposed installation together with a cost estimate. The alternative scheme for road operation should be similarly detailed and priced. Adequate ground, soil and structural surveys should also have been carried out. Sale and lease-back of equipment purchased with the aid of a grant requires the Department's prior approval because it constitutes a change of ownership. Where capital facilities are to be acquired by means of a leasing arrangement grant is normally paid directly to the lessor and the benefits through reduced leasing charges passed to the lessee.

Grants are also available from other sources e.g. the Local Employment Act 1972 and the Industrial Development Act 1982 which provide general powers to Local Authorities by which they can provide assistance to industry if in the local interest: in general a grant will not normally be paid from more than one UK source. There is also a grant scheme from the European Regional Development Fund: the DoT can give details. If the project owner believes that the project cannot go ahead without a grant the authorities to talk to are:

- the Department of Transport
- local authorities to ask for support of the application
- British Rail and Inland Waterway Authorities
- county and district councils for their support

It is essential to have planning permission before discussion of a grant.

The above information has been adapted from the Department of Trade and Industry papers on the subject of grants with permission of the Controller of Her Majesty's Stationery Office.

Further information can be obtained from:

Department of Transport
Railways Directorate
2 Marsham Street, London SW1P 3EB

Scottish Development Department
New St Andrew's House
St James's Centre Edinburgh EH1 3SZ

Welsh Office
Government Buildings
Ty Glas Road
Llanishen Cardiff CF4 5PL

Road access

Although access by road to a site is a prime consideration for some industrial developers the DoT is concerned that access to a premises should not be a danger to road users. The DoT Roads and Local Transport Directorate has issued an Advice Note TA/4/80 'Access to Highways – Safety Implications' which stresses that access to 'trunk and principal roads and all new roads' should be strictly avoided throughout. Developments which increase the use of existing accesses on to existing dual carriageways should also be resisted. The DoT says that accesses were the most important factor contributing to accidents after traffic volumes. Research into access accidents as mentioned in the above Advice Note show that they are in the same proportion in rural as in urban areas.

Since access from a main road is likely to be resisted the alternative is to have access from a minor road which leads into a main road. The problems then are:

- Is the minor road wide enough and strong enough to be used during the construction of the project and afterwards when the site is developed?
- Are there any weak bridges, low bridges, awkward turnings and difficult junctions to be met?
- Are the roads suitable for articulated vehicles?
- Are these local roads well maintained, what is the condition of the roads in winter, are they snowbound or subject to flooding?
- Are the local road routes used by many others and could increased traffic cause delays?
- Would traffic jams be caused by staff arriving and leaving the site mornings and evenings?

Consultation with the local authority is needed to ascertain whether any additional works are needed and if so who is to pay for them. For this investigation a topographical map or even an aerial photograph could be helpful.

If agreement has been reached with the local authority that access may be made and planning permission will not be withheld, advice on access design is given in a publication from the Freight Transport Association, Tunbridge Wells, TN4 9UZ 'Designing for Deliveries' October 1983. This publication includes the design of accesses with due allowance for the path-width of turning goods vehicles and the sight distances necessary for operational safety. If the access is into a two-way highway articulated vehicles turning into the site require special provision in the layout of entry so that the turning vehicle does not impede traffic in the opposite direction. Should access to the site be solely by road the local authority may require adequate parking space for cars and goods vehicles. For some industries visitors are required to park their vehicle outside the factory gates. Lorries arriving may also need to be inspected before entering and this may need to be done in an area where unloading can be carried out under secure conditions. Such conditions require additional space.

Public footpaths

If a prospective site looks acceptable but a public footpath or right of way crosses the land the local authority may allow a rerouting around the property perimeter – at the purchaser's expense – and the cost of maintaining this new path should also be allowed for when comparing costs of sites.

Access to a sea or river port

If access to a waterway or coastal port is essential it would be advisable to discuss the project and material to be handled with local officials. Information would be needed on types and capacity of cranage, whether container vessels can be used, port congestion, and whether dockers are unionized or free. If storage is needed, what facilities are available and what are the storage costs? Docking and handling charges should be investigated. Access to the port by road and rail should be inspected at the busiest times.

Chapter 5

OBTAINING PLANNING PERMISSION

Denis F. McCoy

Making a planning application is a deceptively simple exercise – obtaining planning permission is frequently fraught with difficulty. Sound professional advice and wide experience often need to be brought to bear on preparation of applications if consents are to be secured.

Exploratory research is rarely avoidable. The results should inform selection both of the location of the site for proposed development and its extent if problems of obtaining planning permission are to be minimized.

The history of decisions on and around sites under consideration is obtained by investigation of the planning register which local planning authorities maintain. Though much about the development history of a locality can be assessed from a visit, it is often the invisible factors, i.e. the refusals of permission and the dismissed planning appeals, which are particularly informative. This work can ensure resources are concentrated on working up proposals only for those sites with most hope of success. Nor should any significant planning application be submitted without consideration of relevant approved or adopted policies.

The development plan system

Policies are found in the development plan for an area and include:

- any structure plan (together with the Secretary of State's (Department of the Environment) notice of approval);
- any alterations to that plan (together with the Secretary of State's notices of approval);

- any local plans (together with copies of the planning authority's resolutions of adoption or the Secretary of State's notices of approval);
- any alterations to those plans (together with copies of the appropriate resolutions of adoption or notices of approval); and
- the old development plan approved under the Town and Country Planning Acts up to and including the Act of 1962.

Shire counties prepare structure plans which have to be approved by the Secretary of State. These take account of government policies and state the policies and general proposals for the development and other use of land in the county. They:

- provide a strategic framework for controlling development;
- indicate the scale of provision to be made and in broad terms the main locations for it;
- indicate the general location of significant individual developments.

Structure plans consist of a written statement and a key diagram and are accompanied by an explanatory memorandum.

Local planning authorities prepare and adopt *local plans* which must conform with the structure plan and are sufficiently clear and precise to guide owners and developers of land.

District councils in the former metropolitan counties are to prepare 'unitary development plans'. As their name suggests these will perform both functions and are to have two distinct parts: the councils are obliged to follow strategic planning guidance given by the Secretary of State. This guidance is of great importance while the unitary development plans are awaited.

Supplementary guidance takes many forms and its usefulness must be assessed each time it is encountered. As it is not formally regulated, experience is needed to weigh its relevance, which can be insignificant. Less frequently the guidance has a promotional content, identifying development the planning authority wish to see carried out. Existence of a 'simplified planning zone' may be discovered where permission is already automatically granted for certain development; or an 'enterprise zone' where additionally some tax benefits are offered to stimulate development. Any urban development corporation established to spearhead the regeneration of an urban area will have been identified at an early stage. Less encouragingly these researches will confirm the extent of three important broad-brush restraints on development:

Green belts – 'Thou shalt not . . .'

Well over 30 years old, these now cover about 11 per cent of England (see Figure 5.1.). They are perhaps the most popular planning device. The initial concept was:

Figure 5.1   *Green belts.*
(Redrawn from the Department of the Environment map of Green Belts. With permission of the Controller of HMSO).

- to check further growth of large built-up areas,
- to prevent towns merging into one another,
- to preserve the special character of a town,

and more recently they are seen as assisting urban regeneration.

Green belts are, where practicable, several miles wide so as to ensure an appreciable rural zone all round the built-up area concerned. In them planning permission is not given, except in very special circumstances, for the construction of new buildings, or the change of use of existing ones other than for agriculture, sport, cemeteries, institutions in extensive grounds, or other uses appropriate to a rural area. It is important to note that only in green belts must developers prove the case for their proposal.

National parks – 'Thou probably shalt not . . .'

By February 1987 ten such areas had been designated, covering 13, 600 sq. km. In them the Secretaries of State for the Environment and for Wales have agreed:

> . . . that in the face of growing pressures stricter development control policies need to be applied in the national parks. Such policies are already more stringent in the parks than in the countryside generally but a further opportunity for strengthening them, where this is thought necessary, will be provided in structure plans, which require the Secretary of State's approval, and in local plans.
>
> (Circular 4/76)

Areas of outstanding natural beauty – 'Thou might . . .'

By February 1987 there were 33 such areas totalling 14, 500 sq. km and the Countryside Commission is considering further designations and extensions. Government policy remains basically as stated in Parliament in 1982:

Major development

The Government agree that, in general, it would be inconsistent with the aims of designation to permit the siting of major industrial and commercial development in AONBs. Only proven national interest and lack of alternative sites can justify any exception. But each individual case must be determined on its merits – that is a fundamental rule of our planning system. We believe the environmental effects of new proposals should be a major consideration in all such circumstances . . .

Minor industrial development

In the AONB context the Countryside Commission draws a distinction between the scope for large and small scale industrial development, and the Government endorse this approach. Modern agriculture is capital intensive and can no longer be looked to as a major source of employment in rural areas. Small industries have a vital role to play here, and the Government's wish to encourage such activities was stressed in a recent circular issued jointly by my Department and the Welsh Office. There may be opportunities for small businesses to take over existing premises – redundant farm buildings, for example – and we believe that, subject to certain safeguards, such opportunities should be seized. Where new building is required in a AONB the Government expect such development to be in sympathy with the architecture and landscape of the area.

The application itself

Basically the application must contain:

- a form provided by the local planning authority
- a plan sufficient to identify the land
- plans and drawings necessary to describe the development
- additional copies not exceeding three
- a certificate defining ownership of the land and confirming the steps taken to notify the owner(s) and/or agricultural tenants about the application (s.27, Town and Country Planning Act 1971).
- The appropriate fee – between £38 and £5700. (s.87, Local Government Planning and Land Act 1980; and Regulations periodically reviewed).

In preparing details prior consultation over such technical matters as access standards and drainage provision is essential so that no avoidable objections of detail interrupt progress of the application. Where approval in principle is sought before preparation of detailed plans, an *outline application* can be made, with siting, design, external appearance, means of access and landscaping reserved for subsequent approval. (Local planning authority may require any further information they consider necessary to enable them to determine the application. They may also request evidence to verify any particulars of information given to them) Town and Country Planning (Applications) Regulations 1988.)

There are categories of development including the following which are considered unneighbourly where the applicant has to certify that the application has been advertised:

- public conveniences

- disposal of waste, scrapyards, winning or working of minerals
- other than minor sewage works
- buildings more than 20 metres high
- slaughter houses, knacker's yards
- dance halls, cinemas, Turkish baths, casinos, stadia
- zoos, kennels, catteries
- race tracks
- cemeteries   (s.26 of the Act and Article 11 of General Development Order 1988).

It should be noted that if a local planning authority mistakenly accepts and purports to process such an application not accompanied by such a certificate, refusing it, the planning inspectorate will turn away any appeal because the application was invalid.

Any application *may* be accompanied by much else – supporting correspondence, press releases, model, videos, photomontages, public meetings, lobbying letters to members of the planning authority etc. These possibilities demand careful evaluation. Lobbying against development can be extensive and professional – national amenity groups have been known to publish sophisticated critical reports on proposals, and communities quickly band together, raise funds and oppose change initially aroused by NIMBY (Not in my back yard) principles. Sensitive public relations work before any application is made (years before for the largest projects) will often be appropriate.

There will be times when promoters of the largest projects will need to influence the preparation or amendment of structure and local plans before making their application.

Since July 1988 European Community Directive Number 85/337 has opened the possibility of an environmental assessment being volunteered by or required from applicants in circumstances set out in the Town and Country Planning (Assessment of Environmental Effects) Regulations 1988, but whose exact limits will only be clarified with case histories. Department of the Environment Circular 15/88 contains comprehensive advice. Early consultation and volunteering an assessment can speed the ultimate decision and may be good general tactics in relations with the local community.

Points to watch

Description of development

Thoughtful precision is required – even punctuation or lack of it can introduce ambiguity. Local authority consultation processes use the wording on the form and it will be apparent that public opposition could be unnecessarily aroused by vague or ambiguous wording. Changes/clarification are possible by agreement with the local planning authority, but undesirable. Appeals are only possible on description of the development applied for which again emphasizes the need for clarity and the most positive wording achievable. The scope of future uses is likely to be affected by what is said and so possible future requirements should be considered.

Definition of site

Precision is again important in enclosing with a red line all land required for the proposed development. Access, drainage and landscaping implications may mean this needs to be more extensive than might at first appear. Other land controlled by the applicant is also disclosed to the planning authority. The potentially harmful effect of an inadequate access area for example becoming apparent at a late stage in processing the application will be obvious. Ownership of all the application site is of course not necessary so long as the appropriate notice is given to other parties.

Changes of use

Since 5 December 1988 permission for alternative uses may be sought by a single planning application. Implementation of one of them no longer prevents change to one of the others without a further permission. This "freedom' only lasts for ten years from the grant of permission. Such changes must not be in breach of any condition or other limitation imposed within the terms of the permission itself. (General Development Order, Schedule 2, Part 3, Class E)

Certificates under s.26 and s.27

It is an offence to issue one which contains a statement which the applicant knows to be false or misleading in a material particular. So is 'recklessly' issuing one which is false or misleading. If a factual error is made in the s.27 procedures it does not necessarily result in a grant of permission being quashed: however it may do so if an affected party moves quickly in applying to the Courts. (*Main* v. *Swansea City Council & others*: Court of Appeal, 27 July 1984: JPEL 558–563, 1985)

While positive thinking is a virtue all documentation and negotiations should reflect the possibility that an appeal to the Secretary of State may be unavoidable before permission is obtained: its conduct can be assisted by having all preliminary steps in the optimum form.

There may be advantages in lodging duplicate applications so that negotiations with the local authority on one may proceed without removing the option of appealing against their failure to reach a decision within eight weeks.

What the authority considers

In dealing with applications for planning permission, Section 29(1) of the Town and Country Planning Act 1971 requires that the authority shall have regard to the provisions of the development plan, so far as material to the application, and to any other material considerations:

> Many development plans were approved several years ago, often several years after they had been prepared, and were based on even earlier information. The policies which they contain, and the assumptions on which they were based, may therefore be out of date and not well related to today's conditions. They cannot be adapted rapidly to changing conditions, and they cannot be expected to anticipate every need or opportunity for economic development that may arise. They should not be regarded as overriding other material considerations, especially where the plan does not deal adequately with new types of development or is no longer relevant to today's needs and conditions – particularly the need to encourage employment and to provide the right conditions for economic growth. However, there is a reciprocal point: where the plan is up-to-date and relevant to the particular proposal, it follows that the plan should normally be given considerable weight in the decision and strong contrary planning grounds will have to be demonstrated to justify a proposal which conflicts with it.
>
> (Planning Policy Guidance 1, January 1988)

Material considerations include:

- employment opportunities
- congestion
- loss of countryside
- pollution
- restoration of derelict land
- conservation of natural or man-made heritage.

When preparing an application and any accompanying material thought should be given to framing it in such a way that all these considerations are respected or at least are not in obvious conflict with the proposal. Similarly, the proposal should fit as far as possible with the aims of established policies.

Securing this may involve including something not essential to the project but known to be of perceived importance to the planning authority. Indeed councils do seek to impose on developers an obligation to carry out works not included in the development, or to confer some right or benefit in return for planning permission: they call it planning gain.

Co-operation is generally the best course so long as what is sought is directly related to the proposed developments and/or needed to allow it to proceed, and fairly reflected to it in scale and kind.

Appeals

However well an application is prepared and negotiated inevitably there will be occasions when a council will not grant the desired planning permission. Then an appeal to the Secretary of State will have to be considered.

Many permissions are obtained after the local planning authority have refused to grant consent or failed to make a decision. The right of appeal is the developer's safeguard.

The reasons for refusals should be scrutinized. Is each clear? Do they rely only on up-to-date policies? Could they be overcome by modifications? Do they reflect excessive local opposition rather than sound planning objections? The answers reveal the strength of the council's position.

Though appeals can be dealt with by the medium of written representations a public local inquiry does give the parties an opportunity to test the material rather more directly, effectively and efficiently, and should always be chosen for that reason.

Additional control in special cases

If listed buildings are to be demolished, altered or extended, a separate consent for the work will be required and is *not* given by any planning permission. (1971 Act, Part IV)

Local planning authorities have a duty to consider the effect of development on the setting of a listed building – in some instances this can involve sites not containing or adjacent to listed buildings. (s.56(3) of 1971 Act)

There have been instances of buildings being 'listed' by the Secretary of State at a late stage in preparation for a scheme of development, with consequent delays in or prevention of its implementation. When planning permission is being sought, or has been obtained, any person may apply to the Secretary of State for a certificate stating that it is not intended to list any building(s) shown in the application plans. Thus if a site contains any interesting buildings the desirability of certainty has to be weighed against the risk of drawing attention to a hitherto overlooked building. Once a certificate is issued the building cannot be listed for 5 years, or be the subject of a building preservation notice issued by the local planning authority. (s.54A, Town and Country Planning Act 1971)

In conservation areas consent has to be separately obtained for the demolition of any but minor buildings, which are listed at paragraph 97 of Circular 8/87.

Chapter 6

RECOMMENDATIONS FOR THE PROCUREMENT OF GROUND INVESTIGATION

J.F. Uff and C.R.I Clayton

The following extract from CIRIA Special Publication 45 is published with CIRIA permission. The full publication is available from CIRIA, 6 Storey's Gate, Westminster, London SW1P 3AU.

Introduction

The purpose of ground investigation

Ground investigation is carried out to obtain information about the nature and condition of the ground. This information is needed by the designer to produce an efficient and economic design for those parts of the permanent works which interact with the ground. It is also likely to be relied on for other purposes (e.g. the design of temporary works and the assessment of construction costs and risks by tendering contractors). Ground investigation thus affects the safety both of site operations and of the completed works.

The accuracy and reliability of the information produced by ground investigation is a matter of economic importance to all those involved in a construction contract. The interests of the employer are paramount, because wrong information may invalidate the design of the works, and because under standard forms of contract, such as the ICE Conditions,[1] the cost of overcoming unforeseen ground conditions is likely to rest with the employer. Geotechnical data cannot be checked or verified in the same way as a structural design. Errors or omissions concerning ground information which are revealed at the stage of excavation for the works are likely to have serious financial consequences, and wrong or inaccurate data which remain undetected may put the whole scheme at risk.

Current problems in ground investigation

There is a general consensus within the ground investigation industry that major problems exist, which are principally:

- low price levels
- insufficient resources devoted to investigation
- work of poor quality.

Recently, several of the most highly regarded ground investigation firms have gone out of business or have drastically reduced their operations, as a result of financial pressure brought about by low price levels.

The problems of quality and reliability of ground investigation have persisted in widely differing economic climates. Thus, while the present recession has exacerbated these problems, the root cause lies deeper. The present situation is not caused by any lack of available engineering expertise. Geotechnical engineers are characterized by unusually high levels of post-graduate education and training.

In recent years, ground investigation work has been placed under even greater economic pressures than other areas of the construction industry. As a result, ground investigation has developed into a low-cost industry which is rapidly losing its ability to retain the necessary resources and expertise to operate effectively. The reasons for this state of affairs are considered in a later section, but the consequences are clear. First, substantial additional and avoidable cost to construction results from inadequate ground investigation; second, the current organization of the ground investigation industry is bound to lead to a proportion of work being second-rate.

The economic importance of ground investigation

The economic importance of adequate ground investigation is demonstrated by a recent TRRL Report[2] based on the analysis of ten major highway construction contracts. For these contracts, the final cost was on average 35 per cent greater than the tender sum, and half of this increase was directly attributable to inadequate planning or interpretation of ground investigation.

No similar statistics are available for the cost of foundation or earthworks failures, but experience shows that the cost of remedial work is often comparable to the original price of the whole project.

Initially, much of this additional expense is met by insurance. But the cost of providing insurance is a direct charge to the industry and ultimately to the employer. Expenditure on ground investigation is typically about 1 per cent of the expected tender value of the main works. There is thus a strong economic case for improving the quality and effectiveness of ground investigation. Any consequent cost increases are likely to be trivial in comparison to likely cost benefits.

The ground investigation industry also has economic importance as an employer at various levels, as a market for UK-based manufacturers of specialist equipment, and as a source of exports. It is important that the industry should maintain high standards to be able to compete in world markets.

Methods of improving ground investigation

In a major survey into the civil engineering industry in 1968, the Harris Report[3] concluded that the root cause of poor quality ground investigation lay in the methods of procurement employed. Despite the strong recommendation that methods of procurement should be improved, they have not changed significantly, and most of the problems identified by the Harris Report remain. One of the objectives of this chapter is to identify those methods of procurement which offer the best prospect for overcoming the current problems of ground investigation.

A further objective is to identify factors which, irrespective of the type of procurement, are likely to lead to better quality work. Much commercial ground investigation has been, and continues to be, carried out to good or adequate standards. Those factors which are considered to be conducive to better quality work may therefore be identified to allow recommendations for improving the effectiveness of all ground investigation.

Employers should be persuaded of the need to pay the proper cost of an adequate investigation. But to spend more money is not in itself a solution. If six boreholes are of poor quality, an increase in number does not improve the investigation, and if a supervising engineer is insufficiently experienced, it does not help to increase the amount of time he spends in supervision. What matters is how and where the money is applied. Successful ground investigation requires both adequate funding and the proper direction of those funds through the choice of an appropriate method of procurement.

Systems of procurement in current use

The main elements which make up a system of procurement are:

- the way in which the contract work is defined
- the method by which an acceptable tender is obtained
- the placing and definition of responsibility.

These elements are discussed in this section.

Definition of contract work

The work to be carried out under a ground investigation contract can be defined in various ways. Usually the choice is between method or end result. Logically, the employer should be concerned only with the end result, provided there are assurances of reliability. But the traditional practice is to concentrate on method, and the great majority of contracts are so arranged. This tends to place undue emphasis on physical work and its quantity. The quality or reliability of the data produced is dependent on the degree of supervision and control.

Where the work is defined by method and quantity, there are two principal ways in which the work may be priced: a bill of quantities, coupled with a specified method of measurement, or a schedule of rates for the provision of plant and personnel. The first method is most common, and it usually involves very detailed breakdown of quantities. However, the specifications attached to these documents are usually insufficiently detailed, so that they permit the rejection of only the most obviously deficient work. Specialist contractors complain that this makes competition unfair and largely meaningless, because it does not operate on the basis of common standards of work.

The second method is preferred by many contractors and consulting engineers, but it is difficult to justify economically. It is used with acknowledged success for important components of investigation work, such as production of the interpretative report (see below).

If the contract work is defined by end result instead of method and quantity, a third means of pricing is possible, namely a lump sum. This may be linked to various methods of adjustment, including incentive payments. The use of a lump sum is considered later.

Methods of obtaining tenders

Rys and Wood[4] have identified a number of different methods of obtaining tenders for ground investigation. They conclude that selective tendering (on a specification and bill of quantities) is the most frequent method of procurement in use in the UK, being widely used by central and local government, statutory undertakers, and many consulting engineering practices. The negotiated contract is sometimes favoured by consultants, and it is often used by clients in manufacturing industries and development. It is only occasionally used by government departments and contractors.

Selective tendering

The wide use of competitive tendering reflects the need for public accountability, which applies to almost all public sector employers. Open tendering (i.e. the invitation of tenders without technical selection or without any limit on numbers) is no longer in common use for ground investigation. It cannot be justified in any class of investigation work, because there is no method of ensuring the competence of the lowest tenderer. The method of tendering generally used is selective tendering, which involves usually six (and often more) tenders being obtained from contractors chosen by the engineer or by the employer, usually on the basis of their reputation, ability to carry out the work, or past performance. The employer is then virtually bound to accept the lowest tender. An alternative system has been suggested whereby the employer is advised to accept the tender nearest to the average of all tenders received. It is considered that this would be unworkable because:

1.   Tenderers would have no rational means of arriving at a price likely to be successful. Any unrealistic tender would unbalance the system
2.   The difference between the lowest tender and the average, and between the average and any other tender, would not necessarily reflect any difference in the quality of the work offered
3.   The system would not encourage efficient tendering, and success would be a matter of chance.

The Harris Report criticized selective tendering, based on price alone as being 'inappropriate to sub-soil investigation'. No other basis for competitive tendering is in common use. The system is more justifiable in term contracts, because the successful contractor will have other incentives on a particular job than mere speed of work.

Negotiated contracts

The negotiated contract is, by its nature, a highly variable form of procurement. Negotiation may take place with one or several contractors, on the basis of price or design of ground investigation, or occasionally on the basis of availability and speed of execution of the work. The Harris Report recommended negotiation, with one or with a small number of firms, as a suitable method for the procurement of ground investigation. Negotiated contracts are most often employed for smaller jobs in the private sector.
   The advantages of negotiation are:

● pressure on price levels is relieved
● the specialist contractor may be given the opportunity to use his expertise in the design of the ground investigation

- he may be brought into the design process for the main works.

The main disadvantage of this method is the difficulty of demonstrating public accountability.

Conditions of contract

Ground investigation is usually carried out under a standard form of contract. The most commonly used forms are those of the Institution of Civil Engineers, being either the 5th edition intended for civil engineering construction work,[1] or the form recently produced for ground investigation,[5] which is based on the 5th edition. Both forms require the designation of an engineer who is assumed to provide a full design for the investigation and to administer and provide all necessary supervision for the work. Under these forms of contract, the contractor is given no responsibility for the design, and his duty of superintendence does not extend to ensuring the suitability of the work.

In practice, the contribution of the engineer may amount to full control of the work. In other cases, the consulting engineer or other design professional (who fulfils the role of the engineer under the contract) may have little or no geotechnical expertise, and the control and direction of the work is then left in the hands of the contractor. This is not reflected in the standard form of contract.

In small contracts, the practice exists of obtaining quotations direct from a specialist contractor without involving a consulting engineer. This may be done with or without negotiation, and by inviting one or more tenders. The ground investigation contractor may be given either a statement of objectives or a broad description of the ground investigation work. No standard form of contract exists for this method of procurement. There is often no specification, but the contractor may offer a standard specification, such as that proposed by the Association of Ground Investigation Specialists.[6] Because there is no supervising engineer, all supervision must come from the contractor.

Placing and defining responsibilities

The contractual arrangements commonly used in ground investigation make it difficult to determine the extent of the responsibilities undertaken by each party: the contractor, the engineer and the employer. In addition, the variability of soil and groundwater makes it difficult to identify the source of any error or omission. These factors, coupled with the practice of defining obligations by reference to activities rather than results, often make it practically impossible to apportion blame. Consequently, where errors or omissions occur, it is difficult to determine who is liable. Claims in respect of unforeseen ground conditions are rarely made against either the specialist ground investigation contractor or the consulting engineer.

In terms of responsibility, the employer is better served by dealing with one contracting party only, so that there is then no doubt about responsibilities. Thus, when a specialist contractor is employed without the use of a consulting engineer (as commonly occurs for small projects), the contractor is bound to assume responsibility for all aspects of the work. That such a system can work well is shown by the frequent use of the arrangement described above.

Current problems of the ground investigation industry

The shortcomings in ground investigation can be viewed as resulting from certain primary causes, which are imposed upon the industry from outside, and also from consequent inadequacies which are, at least in part, the response of the industry to external conditions.

The primary causes include:

- unfair or unsuitable methods of competition
- inappropriate conditions of contract
- insufficient and inadequate supervision
- inadequate and unenforceable specification of work.

Consequent inadequacies include:

- incorrect motivation
- poor continuity and communication
- loss of expertise from the industry
- inadequate education, training and investment.

In 1968, the Harris Report specifically identified methods of competition and conditions of contract as causes of poor ground investigation. Undoubtedly, the problems of supervision and specification applied equally in 1968 as today. Clearly, the consequent inadequacies will not be materially improved until the primary causes are effectively tackled. Since the Harris Report, significant changes have occurred in the state of the ground investigation industry. The most important has been a reduction in workload to around 60 per cent of the peak level. Other significant changes include increased competition from new entrants into the industry (such as local authorities), considerably increased price competition (resulting in even lower prices), and the withdrawal of existing specialists from the industry.

Methods of competition

As was noted earlier, selective tendering is the most widely used method to obtain an acceptable tender. Most ground investigation contracts are let on the basis of detailed rates for boring and drilling, sampling and testing, with lump sums for items such as mobilization and report writing. The cost of fieldwork is typically 60 to 70 per cent of the total cost of ground investigation, so that competitive tendering is, in reality, largely based upon unit rates for fieldwork. The need to reduce overheads so as to remain competitive has meant that many specialist contractors have, in recent years, sold their drilling rigs, re-employed their drillers as self-employed sub-contractors, and reduced their levels of engineering supervision in the field. Investment in plant and training has been minimal, so that drillers continue to work with primitive equipment in hostile and often unsafe conditions. Current methods of competition are thus directly conducive to poor workmanship.

There have been two improvements to the traditional system in recent years. One is the use, in Department of Transport contracts, of rate-only items for engineering time for interpretative report writing, and sometimes for self-supervision by the ground investigation contractor. The other is the use of dayworks schedules to pay for work in more critical areas of the investigation.

There can be no objection to fair competition between tenderers. The present system is poor because it fails to ensure that tenderers price for the same end product, particularly in terms of drilling quality and engineering staff levels. Tight specification, close supervision and enforcement should be capable of overcoming the problem, but in practice these are rarely applied. The Harris Report observed that there was then little scope for reducing prices in ground investigation without seriously impairing the quality of the work. Since that date, prices (in real terms) have been forced down further, such that investigation today is often based on minimum cost and maximum speed, which inevitably increases the risk of poor quality work.

Many ground investigation contractors state that the practice of accepting the lowest of six or more tenders has been the main factor in the decline of quality and profitability in the industry, and that to change this alone would lead to improvements. However, the need for public accountability means that most ground investigation work requires competitive tendering in some form. Despite suggestions to the contrary, competition usually results in acceptance of the lowest tender.

Consulting engineers argue that limited tender lists and careful preselection of tenderers can make competitive tendering a fair and effective process. At present, tender lists are too long. Preselection is not applied systematically, and employers tend to ask for local companies to be placed on tender lists. Preselection does not work unless all tenderers are selected by the same searching criteria.

Conditions of contract

Earlier it was noted that ground investigation is commonly carried out under forms based on the ICE Conditions. These conditions are designed for a situation in which design and construction skills can be effectively separated so that the engineer and contractor play distinct and exclusive roles. The different interests of the engineer and contractor are not detrimental to the proper construction of the permanent work. This is not the case with ground investigation, which depends for its successful implementation on interaction and co-operation between those directing and those performing the investigation, at all stages. Further, the traditional forms of contract used in construction work are based on a clear predefinition of the work content, limited amendments being made after letting the contract. The essence of ground investigation is flexibility of approach, so that the type and amount of work may be redefined as the investigation proceeds.

The fact that much good quality investigation is carried out using the ICE Conditions is more a tribute to the good sense of those carrying out the work than to the Conditions. Given that they are (and will continue to be) used, it remains essential that the engineer should provide the full degree of supervision and expertise assumed under the ICE Conditions. Where this is done, the Conditions can operate adequately in practice. But where the engineer cannot provide full control, or where it is desired to use the engineering expertise of the contractor, other means of procurement should be used (see below).

Specification of work

In contracts based on quantities of work, a particular problem which faces the supervisor on site is the need for adequate and relevant technical specifications. Such documents are difficult to draft, but they are essential. Specifications should define the limits of accuracy and of quality for materials. They should also cover the equipment to be used, and give detailed method statements which can be readily enforced by the supervisor. Few, if any, of the documents in common use can be considered adequate for their purpose.

In the absence of properly defined specifications and standards, and without adequate enforcement through supervision, the standard of investigation work produced is unpredictable, and it often depends on the amount of skill, expertise and supervision which the contractor is able or prepared to give. Thus, 'competitive' tenders based on unit rates have no common base, and the result is, as observed by the Harris Report, that 'the client usually gets what he pays for'. In other words, the lower the tendered price, the lower the standard of the investigation which the contractor can provide for that price.

Supervision

In the circumstances which currently exist in the industry, supervision is vital to the achievement of good quality work. Although no distinction is drawn in the ICE forms of contract or in the Association of Consulting Engineers (ACE) Conditions,[7] the type and degree of supervision required in ground investigation is quite different from that required during a construction project. In the latter case, it is generally sufficient that supervision should detect any defect in the finished work before it is covered up. In ground investigation, supervision should, ideally, be continuous if non-compliance is to be detected. For example, a good quality standard penetration test requires attention not only to the test equipment and method of test, but also to the method of boring to reach the test location, the position of casing relative to the bottom of the boring, and the water levels within the boring, before and during the test. The end product is a number, the validity of which can be known only if all these matters have been observed, reported, and considered.

Supervision of ground investigation can thus be carried out only while the work is in progress. For supervision to be effective, the person to whom it is entrusted should:

- be fully aware of the aims of the investigation and the expected ground conditions
- be experienced and competent in the field and laboratory techniques in use
- have delegated powers to alter the size and scope of the investigation as it proceeds.

This role cannot be fulfilled by a trainee or a junior member of staff. In ground investigation, supervision must ensure adequate quality and compliance with standards, and it should provide critical interpretation of the samples and data as they emerge, in order to allow the proper direction of the investigation.

In the great majority of work undertaken, supervision is inadequate both in terms of the quantity and quality of staff available on site. Proper supervision and insistence on adequate standards of work are likely to make it impossible for contractors who tender at low rates to complete their contracts without making a substantial loss.

Consequent inadequacies

There is a general problem of continuity and communication between the parties involved in ground investigation. As the number of activities which are sub-contracted increases, and the retention of qualified staff becomes more difficult, there is a growing problem of fragmentation in the industry. This can have a direct effect on the quality of the work produced, because the production of a reliable report requires communication between all the parties involved at different stages of the investigation. Interpretation of data starts at a very basic level (e.g. a drilling foreman initiates the process of interpretation when he divides the ground into strata, or assesses the inflow of water to a hole). Failure to communicate with other members of the team means that significant information may be lost.

A ground investigation report is likely to be used for several different purposes. These include the design of permanent structural works, earthworks and temporary works, as well as the assessment of construction conditions. All these aspects have important financial consequences for the client and for others. There is often failure at the planning stage to appreciate these different needs, and to advise the client that it is in his interest that they should all be adequately covered by the investigation.

Investigation work is usually carried out in advance of construction. The person responsible for geotechnical investigations and recommendations is rarely available to communicate with those carrying out either design or construction. Therefore he is unable either to assist the designer or the general contractor for the main works in interpreting the data or to learn from his previous mistakes. Greater involvement and identification of individuals is desirable. There should be an identified, experienced, well qualified geotechnical engineer associated with every project from conception to completion. Where such a person cannot be provided from the clients staff or by the ground investigation contractor or design professional, an independent geotechnical specialist should be brought in.

Improving the ground investigation process

Having reviewed the way in which ground investigation is carried out in terms of organization and performance, it may be stated that the industry remains capable of producing work to the high standards required by the construction industry. But such standards are only likely to be achieved when the parties (particularly the employer) are able to select an appropriate system of procurement.

Ensuring a complete and well designed ground investigation

A good ground investigation requires the following steps:

- retention of a competent geotechnical adviser at an early stage
- adequate desk study and inspection of the site
- considered initial design of the investigation, taking into account the probable ground conditions and the structure to be built
- definition of proper standards of work

- enforcement of those standards during investigation
- assessment of ground conditions as work proceeds
- redirection and reassessment of initial intentions as work proceeds
- design of relevant laboratory testing programmes
- proper and continuous interpretation of data.

A successful system of procurement is one which results in each of these activities being given proper attention. Where consulting engineers are engaged to control the work, the initial stages of the investigation are their responsibility. The job of carrying out the field and laboratory work to proper standards rests with the contractor. Where more than one party is to participate in the work, there is a risk either that there will be duplication of effort, or that some activities may be omitted. It is essential to have a clear definition of the work to be undertaken by each party.

Whatever the method of procurement, the identification by the client of an organization with sufficient geotechnical skill is an essential first step towards good ground investigation. It is not easy for many clients to identify sources of geotechnical skill. There is a need for publication of a list, to be updated regularly, which sets out the names of:

1. individual geotechnical specialists with addresses, professional and academic qualifications, and current employer
2. consulting engineering practices employing geotechnical specialists with approximate size of geotechnical group
3. specialist contractors with approximate number of geotechnical specialists.

To be regarded as a geotechnical specialist, a person should have relevant practical experience together with qualifications, which should include the status of Chartered Engineer or Member of the Institution of Geologists. Postgraduate qualifications in particular areas of geotechnical engineering (soil mechanics, rock mechanics, foundation engineering or engineering geology) should be taken into account.

The task of preparing such a list is being undertaken by the British Geotechnical Society.

Choice of a system of procurement

It is evident that there are, potentially, many ways in which ground investigation could be adequately procured. The practical need is to identify systems which embody the best current practices and which are capable of refinement so as to achieve the objectives set out above. It is also desirable to keep to a minimum the number of systems which need to be considered by clients when commissioning investigation work. These considerations lead to the definition of two broad systems of procurement:

- *System 1* – design of the investigation and supervision by a consulting engineer or other design professional employed by the client, physical work, testing and reporting being carried out as required under a separate contract by a contractor, chosen by selective tendering.
- *System 2* – design and direction, together with all physical work, testing and reporting as required, by a single contracting party in a 'package' arrangement made with the employer.

The essential distinction between these two systems is that the first adheres to traditional methods in construction, and it may be said to have grown out of the existing structure of the industry, while the second embodies greater flexibility and is closer to the recommendation of the Harris Report that ground investigation should be treated as a professional service.

System 1 has the advantage of using well known forms of contract, and it can demonstrate cost accountability through the tendering process. It also allows the design engineer to participate in the investigation process. Its disadvantages include the difficulty of ensuring that adequate expertise and supervision are provided by the engineer, and the effects of competitive tendering.

System 2 is capable of overcoming these problems, and it allows full use to be made of the expertise of the specialist contractor. It also avoids any division or confusion of responsibilities, but there is less available experience in the use of System 2, particularly in large contracts.

The two systems are now considered in more detail to identify the essential requirements for their successful use.

System 1

This system is well established in practice, using existing tendering procedures and forms of contract. The client enters into two separate contracts, with a consulting engineer for the design and supervision of the investigation (typically the ACE Conditions[7]), and with a contractor for the physical work, testing, and reporting (under either the ICE 5th edition[1] or the ICE Conditions[5]). The requirements for successful use of this system are:

1. The supervising engineer (the engineer's representative) must have sufficient experienced staff to carry out the duties placed on him, particularly with regard to the design of the ground investigation and the supervision of work on site and in the laboratory
2. The engineer's conditions of engagement should spell out the need for proper levels of supervision. They should also provide for appropriate payment

3. Careful attention should be paid to preselection to ensure the use of a competent and well resourced contractor
4. The tender list should be restricted to an absolute maximum of six carefully selected firms
5. Particularly critical work should be paid for under dayworks schedules,[8] or on a time basis
6. Detailed site-specific specifications should be used which readily allow the identification of work of unacceptable quality.

The first requirement, the capability of the supervising engineer, demands careful selection by the client of either a general civil engineering consultant with specialist geotechnical staff of sufficient quality and number to carry out the work, or the use of a specialist geotechnical consultant. The enforcement of standards, assessment of ground conditions during investigation, redirection of the work, and proper interpretation of data all require skilled and constant supervision.

In North America, good practice requires one trained supervisor at each drilling rig, or perhaps one supervisor for two drilling rigs on compact sites. Without this level of supervision, it is impossible to ensure that standards are maintained, and that sampling and *in situ* testing are relevant to the ground conditions. If senior staff are not to be deployed on site and in the laboratory, there is a need to train specialist technical supervisors and to provide adequate communication with superiors. They should also be properly briefed before each investigation, to ensure that they understand the expected ground conditions, the requirements of the structure which is to be erected, and the implications of any unexpected features they may encounter. Correct levels of supervision will mean a considerable increase in the cost of the service provided by consulting engineers.

The requirement for proper levels of supervision is a matter solely between the engineer and his client. It is difficult for the engineer (who may himself be required to tender in competition) to convince the client of the need for additional cost, particularly because this is usually outside the ACE Conditions. The supervision duties taken on need to be clarified: this may be done by special conditions written into the appointment of the engineer. In any case where the client does not sanction adequate payment for supervision, where a proper level of supervision is considered uneconomic, or where the engineer does not have geotechnical expertise sufficient to carry out adequate design and supervision, System 1 is not appropriate, and should not be used.

The selection of a competent contractor is vital, whatever system of procurement is used. The compilation of a list of suitable tenderers requires geotechnical knowledge and experience of the previous performance of the companies under consideration. During preselection, visits should be made to each contractor's office, laboratories, and sites. Attention should be paid to the level of resources available (rigs, laboratory and field testing equipment, special facilities, etc.) and to the qualifications, experience and length of service with the contractor of his engineers, technicians, field supervisory staff, and drilling foremen. The standard of routine reporting on previous jobs by drillers, technicians and engineers should be examined.

The number of tenderers selected should normally not exceed four, with an absolute limit of six. The geotechnical adviser should recommend and agree with the client which companies are to be included in the tender list. This decision should not be overridden by non-specialists.

The clear definition of proper standards of work is essential when employing competitive tendering. It also allows contractors who carry out good quality work to be recognized. Tenders are not on a common base unless there is a specification which allows supervisors to reject poor workmanship. The ground investigation industry requires a national standard specification. BS 5930[9] is not a specification, and other current British Standards include specifications for only a few individual components of ground investigation (e.g. the standard penetration test). A ground investigation specification, published in parts (periodically revised) dealing with separate aspects, should provide precise details of equipment, dimensions, tolerances and materials. It should also specify calibration requirements and provide detailed method statements for such activities as boring and drilling, sampling, *in situ* testing, the formation of piezometers, and the laboratory testing of samples.

A dayworks schedule for standard site operations is available[8] for use with the ICE Conditions.[5] This approach can be used to pay for critical fieldwork, where it is desirable to avoid the pressure to recover overheads by rapid working. In addition, bills of quantities may include items (with provisional quantities) to allow the engineer to order the use of plant, equipment or personnel at hourly or daily rates, so as to permit close direction of key parts of the investigation.

The preparation of a geotechnical report is a vital aspect of any investigation. The report represents the culmination of the work, and it forms the permanent record which may be consulted and relied on many years after other records and evidence have been dispersed.

The geotechnical report presents the factual data from the investigation, and it usually includes an interpretative section which may contain specific advice on the design or construction of the permanent works. Under System 1, the contractor usually produces the factual part of the report. The use of System 1 implies that the supervising engineer possesses such a level of expertise that it is desirable for him to produce the interpretative report. The supervising engineer should always retain overall responsibility for the final report presented to the client. However, it may be appropriate to ask the contractor to prepare interpretative material to be incorporated into the final report, where he possesses particular expertise or where the expertise or experience of the supervising engineer is limited.

It is considered desirable for specialist contractors to be assured of a reasonable volume of interpretative report writing in order to maintain their levels of engineering expertise. This practice may also improve the self-supervision and quality control applied by the contractor. Whoever prepares the interpretative report, it is particularly desirable that this work should be paid for on a time basis. This has been successfully adopted by some government departments.

System 2

In this system, the employer enters into one contract which embraces design of the investigation, its direction, and the physical work required. The principal difference from traditional methods is that, under System 2, there is no pre-arranged design for the investigation. The selected specialist prepares his own design for the investigation using his own expertise, which may include knowledge of the site in question. The system allows competitive tendering between a number of specialists, but competition is then on the basis of design rather than drilling rates. The employer has the advantage of considering alternative proposals for the achievement of an adequate investigation.

There is no separately engaged consulting engineer under System 2. The employer may need to engage the services of an independent geotechnical adviser to assist in the preselection of tenderers and in the assessment of tenders. The geotechnical adviser may also be asked to act as supervisor of the work. A potential disadvantage of System 2 is that the main works design engineer is not directly involved in the direction of the investigation. However, if he has the necessary expertise, he may act as the independent geotechnical adviser. As part of the work in the package, the employer may also include a requirement to produce design proposals for the permanent works.

Arrangements corresponding to System 2 are currently used in a variety of forms, both in ground investigation and more extensively in construction work. The system has the obvious advantage of eliminating duplication of effort and cost, and of avoiding disputes between those who direct and those who perform the physical work. A disadvantage is that there is no accepted form of contract for ground investigation, but there are available precedents to allow a suitable form to be prepared. A major advantage of System 2 is that it allows non-specialist design professionals, including architects, to procure adequate ground investigation without themselves taking on duties which they are unqualified to perform.

System 2 follows procedures developed in general construction work. At present, package-deal ground investigation is mainly restricted to either smaller or overseas projects. For larger projects, there is a clear need to establish a standardized procedure.

The following points should be noted:

1. Because each tenderer is invited to submit his own design, there is need

for a careful preselection process. Not more than three tenderers should be selected. Where neither the employer nor his design professional possesses geotechnical skill, it may be necessary (in the absence of previous experience of ground investigation) to employ a geotechnical consultant to carry out preselection

2. Tenders should be submitted in a predetermined common format to facilitate analysis and comparison. The employer may require specialist geotechnical advice on the assessment of tenders, although the preselection process normally allows acceptance of the lowest bid

3. Although certain administrative functions are carried out by the design professional or by a representative of the employer (i.e. the supervisor), the specialist who carries out the work is fully responsible for both the design of the investigation and the supervision of its execution

4. Because a System 2 contract involves both design and execution of ground investigation, it is appropriate for the specialist to be required to give a warranty for the benefit of the employer. The draft form of contract contains a warranty of reasonable skill and care, which expresses no more than the duty undertaken at common law by any professional firm or contractor. The warranty expressly covers all the work to be undertaken, including the report. An optional limitation of liability is also provided.

Under System 2, the specialist may be either a specialist geotechnical consultant or a general civil engineering consultant, using sub-contractors for drilling and laboratory testing. Equally, the specialist may be a specialist ground investigation contractor, using *ad hoc* geotechnical consultants where necessary. Where two organizations combine to act as the specialist, there will be only one contract, placed with the consortium.

Variants on System 1

The usual application of System 1 involves the engagement of a large consulting civil engineering practice with a specialist geotechnical team to provide all necessary design and supervisory expertise. Where the design professional does not have the necessary expert resources, and System 1 is to be used, a specialist geotechnical consultant must be brought in, to be directly employed by the client or by the design professional. The essence of System 1 is that the contractor, while being expected to be skilled in field and laboratory techniques, is not required to design the investigation or to provide close supervision of site work. Consequently, in some cases it will be appropriate to use contractors without strong geotechnical backing. In larger contracts, however, it is expected that the larger specialist firms will be included in the tender list, and their available expertise may be called on in particular instances by the controlling engineer.

Although the form of contract used with this system is normally either the ICE 5th edition or the Conditions[5] there is no necessary or desirable standard for the contract documents to be used in System 1. Modified forms of the ICE 5th edition are known to be used satisfactorily. A full and adequate specification is vital in this form of contract. Standardization of the way in which the work content of the contract is defined (i.e. using bills of quantities and a standard method of measurement) is less vital, because the work is closely controlled and directed by the engineer.

Variants on System 2

By its nature, a package contract encompasses many possible arrangements, including the provision of all necessary services by one party (usually a specialist contractor), or the provision of design and supervisory services by one party and the provision of site and laboratory services by another (i.e. by consultants and contractors, respectively). The way in which the service is divided between the participants is immaterial, because there is one indivisible contract with the employer.

Under System 2, there may be variants in the contract documents and in the method of obtaining an acceptable tender. Thus, for smaller projects, there is a common practice of obtaining a single proposal from a specialist contractor for an investigation. This may be based on a lump sum, a schedule of rates, or bills of quantities. There is no recognized form of contract in this type of work. The apparent success of the system suggests that none is needed where a single tenderer is asked to quote for a comparatively small or straightforward project. However, where multiple tenders are to be invited, or where the project is larger or more complex, the formalities in System 2 become necessary for the protection of both employer and specialist.

System 2 can be used with a system of remeasurement of the work actually carried out, instead of a lump-sum price. Some specialists have expressed preference for this. However, it is considered that such an arrangement would be difficult to justify in terms of accountability, and the obligation to pay for the cost of changes to the original proposals would lead to greater involvement by the supervisor to protect the employer's interest. A refusal to sanction recommended changes would also reduce the value of the warranty given by the specialist. Many specialist contractors have worked successfully under lump-sum package arrangements. This undoubtedly reflects the demands of the market now and in the future, both in the UK and abroad.

If it is desired to introduce into a package contract means of adjustment to the fixed price, there are numerous precedents available in the form of target or bonus arrangements which have been worked out for construction contracts. It is considered that such devices would be preferable to introducing remeasurement of the quantities of work performed. However, the general rule applying to System 2 contracts should be that a simple lump sum is used, so that the success of the specialist depends on his expertise and skill and not on his ability to gain advantage from the terms of a necessarily complex contractual document.

Notes

1. Institution of Civil Engineers, *Conditions of contract and forms of tender, agreement and bond for use in connection with works of civil engineering construction*, 5th edition, 1973.
2. Tyrrell, A.P., Lake, L.M. and Parsons, A.W., *An investigation of the extra costs arising on highway contracts*, Transport and Road Research Laboratory, Crowthorne, Berks, Supplementary Report 814, 1983.
3. Economic Development Committee for Civil Engineering, *Contracting in civil engineering since Banwell*, Report of the Working Party, under the chairmanship of W.G. Harris, HMSO, London, 1968.
4. Rys, L.J. and Wood, I.R., 'A question of priority – product before procurement' in *Site investigation practice: assessing BS 5930* Proc. 20th Reg. Meeting of the Engineering Group of the Geological Society held at University of Surrey, 1984, The Geological Society, London, 1986.
5. Institution of Civil Engineers, *ICE Conditions of Contract for Ground Investigation*, Thomas Telford Ltd, London, 1983.
6. Association of Ground Investigation Specialists, 'Specification for ground investigations', *Ground Engineering* July 1979 **12**(5), pp.56–67.
7. Association of Consulting Engineers, *ACE Conditions of Engagement*, ACE, London, 1981.
8. Federation of Civil Engineering Contractors, *Standard site operations Daywork Schedule for inclusion in bills of quantities for contracts under the ICE Conditions of Contract for Ground Investigation*, FCEC, London, 1984.
9. British Standards Institution, *Code of practice for site investigations BS 5930*: 1981.

Chapter 7

COMMENTS ON THE INSTITUTION OF CIVIL ENGINEERS CONDITIONS OF CONTRACT FOR GROUND INVESTIGATION*

D.G. Valentine

The legal background

Formation of the contract

The contract is formed by:

- the contractor's tender;
- the employer's acceptance

If the contractor qualifies his tender in a covering letter, his letter will have no effect if the acceptance is of 'the tender' because acceptance of the tender is not acceptance of the covering letter.

* Copies of the Conditions may be obtained from the Secretary, The Institution of Civil Engineers, 1–7 Great George Street, London SW1P 3AA, price £4.00. The copyright of the Conditions is held by the ICE.

If the covering letter is incorporated into the tender, then an acceptance of the tender is an acceptance of the tender as qualified by the covering letter.

A letter of intent is not an acceptance of the tender and has no legal effect at all. If the letter of intent requests work to be done by the contractor, and he expressly or by implication agrees to do that work, a mini-contract is formed by the request and this express or implied agreement. That contract has nothing to do with the ICE Conditions.

The acceptance of the tender, with or without acceptance of the covering letter, must be unqualified. If the acceptance is conditional – such as an acceptance provided the relevant planning permission is forthcoming – then the acceptance is only effective when the condition has been satisfied and the contractor knows that this is so.

The form of agreement

When entered into, the form of agreement prescribed by the ICE does not produce a contract, because a contract has already been formed by the tender and its acceptance. The agreement merely sets out in a formal manner what has already been agreed.

Limitation periods

1. If English law applies to the contract, the contractor is liable for breaches of contract for six years from the date of the breach, or for twelve years from the date of the breach if the agreement is under seal.
2. If the site is in Scotland, Scots law applies (Clause 67). Under Scots law the period for suing for breach of contract is five years from the date of the breach, or twenty years from the date of the breach if the agreement is under seal.
3. The contractor, and any sub-contractor, is liable in tort in negligence. If physical injury results from that negligence the period for bringing a legal action is three years from the date of the injury. If damage to property results, the period is six years from the date when the damage occurred. In addition, in England and Wales an action can be brought for three years from the date when that damage could first reasonably have been discovered, if this is later. Except in Scotland, no action in tort lies, however, more than fifteen years after the date of the negligence.
4. The defects liability period is the first year (or six months) of the six or twelve (or in Scotland five or twenty) years' liability referred to above.

    When all defects notified to the contractor have been rectified, and completion certificates issued in respect of all laboratory testing and all the parts, the engineer issues the acceptance certificate. This certificate, however, has no effect on the liability of the contractor or the employer. (See Clause 61(2).)

The engineer's obligations

Supervision and administration

Except in the case of life and death, the engineer owes no duty to the contractor to tell him that he has gone wrong – see, for example, clause 17, last sentence.

The engineer's duties are to see that the investigation is carried out in accordance with the contract. These duties are owed to the employer not the contractor.

If defects in the ancillary works appear, the engineer has power under Clause 39(1) to order the rectification or the removal and proper re-execution of any defective work. This clause is not applicable to slipshod methods of boring or of testing. In those cases the engineer has to operate under his wide powers under Clause 13(1).

Variation orders

Ancillary work

In respect of the permanent work (ancillary work) required to be constructed, variation orders can require additions or omissions, and so on.

Boring

In respect of boring and so on, variation orders can add or omit boreholes. They can also alter the method, timing or sequence of taking the boreholes – provided that this method, timing or sequence was set out in the specification.

If it was not so set out, the engineer can still in effect change the contractor's method of making boreholes by withholding his consent to the contractor's proposed methods – Clause 14(3) – or by withholding his approval under Clause 13(2).

If the sequence of the boring has not been specified, that sequence can probably be altered under Clause 13(1) – although the wording is not clear. Cost incurred as a result of such alteration, if it can be effected, would be due under both Clauses 13(3) and 14(6).

Laboratory tests

The engineer can order additional tests or he can omit tests and so on, and change the specified method, timing or sequence of those tests.

Draft and final reports

On its strict wording, the variation clause is wide enough to allow the engineer to order additions, omissions, substitution and alterations to the draft and final reports.

If any of these variations affected the meaning or impact of the reports, a strong contractor would refuse to comply – thereby placing himself in breach of Clause 13(1), but with no damages being incurred by the employer.

A weak contractor would comply with the variation order and leave it to the employer to claim any redress from the engineer who ordered the variations.

Nominations

The engineer has power to nominate a person to carry out work within a prime cost item – Clause 58(4).

If he does so nominate, the contractor can refuse the nomination if he has reasonable grounds for so doing, or if the sub-contractor refuses to take on the same obligations to the contractor as the contractor owes to the employer.

No one can say whether the contractor's refusal is reasonable; the engineer, therefore, does not know whether he has a duty to renominate – Clause 59A(2) (a) – or to hold the contractor in breach under Clause 13(1) for not complying strictly with an engineer's instruction.

Further, if the nominated contractor carries out defective work, the employer, by way of damages, cannot recover from the contractor any sum greater than that which the contractor can recover from the sub-contractor.

Thus if a nominated sub-contractor goes into liquidation and is not worth suing, the employer himself pays for the rectification of all that nominated sub-contractor's defective work.

Had the relevant work not been made a prime cost item, so that consequently there had been no nomination, the contractor would have had to have the relevant work carried out by a domestic sub-contractor. If that sub-contractor goes into liquidation, it is the contractor, not the employer, who has to pay to correct defects.

Delegation to the engineer's representative

The engineer can delegate certain of his powers to the engineer's representative, but not powers to extend time (Clause 44), to take decisions on unforeseen site conditions (Clause 12) or to give a decision on appeal under Clause 66.

Notice of the delegation must be sent to the contractor (Clause 2(3)).

The contractor can appeal to the engineer against any instruction of the engineer's representative. The engineer must then confirm, reverse or vary the instruction.

The contractor's obligations

Carrying out the investigations

The contractor's basic obligation is to carry out the investigation, which is divided into four stages:

1. Boring, designing trial pits etc. on site, and backfilling
2. Constructing permanent erections on site. The erections are called 'ancillary works'
3. Carrying out laboratory tests
4. Preparing the draft and final reports.

Stages 1 and 2 are collectively defined in 'site operations'.

The contractor's methods for carrying out the investigation must be approved by the engineer (Clause 14(3)).

Boring etc.

The contractor is responsible for the safety of all operations (Clause 15(1)). He is to provide suitably qualified staff including those qualified to describe soil and rock and to log trial pits and so on (Clauses 15(1) and (3)). He is responsible for the care and storage of samples.

If the contractor is to carry out backfilling of trial pits and so on, any subsidence of the backfilling is to be rectified during the period of maintenance.

Ancillary works

If the contractor is required to construct permanent work on the site, the contract is run just as under the ICE 5th edition, with provision for variations, with rectifications to be carried out during the period of maintenance, and so on.

Laboratory tests

The samples and cores obtained by the contractor are to be tested only in laboratories approved by the engineer – (Clause 1(1)). The nature of these tests can be set out in the specification; if not, the engineer is to approve the contractor's proposed testing schedule (Clause 14(4)).

The contract refers to the draft report and the final report. The format of these can either be specified or left to the contractor.

The investigation will usually have been commissioned with some type of development in mind. Specific characteristics of the soil, such as its strata, its acidity and bearing strength, will be awaited. This will determine the scope of the investigation and the content of the reports.

The draft report and the final report are to be sent to the engineer for his approval (Clause 14(5)). The time allowed for such approval is to be set out in the appendix to the tender.

What the engineer is approving is not stated. Presumably, the engineer is to satisfy himself, for example, that the data obtained are adequate for a conclusion and recommendation to be made and that all soil characteristics asked for have been described.

On general principles, the engineer's approval presumably has no effect on the contractor's liability for inaccurate descriptions or for badly conducted tests. Clause 14(6) states that the engineer's approval of the contractor's programme or his methods does not relieve the contractor of any of his duties or responsibilities.

Presumably by an oversight, this clause has not been widened to cover also approval of the draft or final report.

Design

By this contract a contractor can be required merely to take, say, ten cores at defined positions; to describe and test those cores and issue a report. His contractual obligations are then to carry out these duties with all reasonable skill and care. The contractor is liable in damages for any breach of these duties.

Alternatively, the contractor can be asked merely to provide certain information and, perhaps, recommendations in a report. It is then left entirely to the contractor to carry out such boring, or sink such trial pits and carry out such tests as he thinks necessary to enable the information to be given and the recommendation to be competently made.

If the recommendations are incorrect, is the contractor in breach of contract?

The answer will depend on whether the incorrect recommendations are the result of cores being badly taken or improperly described, or the tests being inappropriate or badly conducted.

Suppose, however, the recommendations are wrong because, say, boreholes sunk at points A, B and C gave certain readings justifying the recommendations, whereas if the boreholes had been sunk at X, Y and Z, they would have given different readings – in the light of which 'correct' recommendations would have been given.

The issue then is: would a competent soil investigator, acting competently, have been satisfied with only three boreholes? If so, was he justified to place the boreholes at points A, B and C, or does anything in the layout of the land indicate that at least one borehole should have been in the region of X, Y or Z? If one or more boreholes had been in that region, would they have revealed anything to lead a competent contractor to alter his recommendations?

Alternatively, if a competent soil investigator had sunk a minimum of more than three boreholes, was there anything indicating to that investigator that some of these additional boreholes should have been sunk in the region of X, Y or Z? Again, if they had been, what would have been revealed?

Further factors in determining the contractor's liability are whether there was any price restraint placed on the contractor by the employer, and whether the contractor skimped the work in order to get the job.

Time

The period within which the investigation must be completed is to be set out in the appendix to the tender. This can be fixed either by the engineer, or by the contractor.

The investigation can be split into sections either relating to defined areas of the site; or into stages of the work, e.g. boring, laboratory tests, ancillary work, and reports.

The site operations (boring and so on, plus ancillary work) can be given their own period for completion, and these operations can be subdivided into further sections.

All these minutiae make administering the contract unnecessarily difficult.

The contractor's programme

Within 21 days of the acceptance of the tender, the contractor is required to submit his programme to the engineer for approval (Clause 14(1)).

Nothing is stated about what happens if the engineer does not approve the programme.

Date for commencement

The engineer is to notify the contractor of the date for commencement. This date is to be within a reasonable time after the date of the acceptance of the tender (Clause 41). The completion period runs from this date for commencement (Clause 43).

Extension of time

The grounds for extensions

There are five grounds for extending time:

1. Variation orders
2. Quantities exceeding those stated in the bills of quantities
3. Delays referred to in the conditions of contract, i.e. those caused by:
    *   unforeseen ground conditions – Clause 12(3);
    *   unforeseen instructions from the engineer – Clause 13(3);

- engineer's delay in giving approvals – Clause 14(4) and (5);
- compliance with highway regulations – Clause 27(6);
- unexpected facilities being required for other contractors – Clause 31(2);
- suspension orders – Clause 40(1);
- non-possession of site – Clause 42(1);
- lawful dismissal of nominated sub-contractors – Clause 59B(4) (b)

4.   Exceptional adverse weather conditions
5.   Other special circumstances of any kind whatsoever.

Ground 5 is very wide: there is no authority upon what is included within it.

Extending time

The engineer must on four occasions consider what is the period of the extension of time that is due to the contractor:

1.   During the execution of the investigation (whether or not the contractor has applied for any extension)
2.   When liquidated damages first became due
3.   On the issue of the certificate of completion
4.   Upon any reference of a dispute concerning time referred to the engineer under Clause 66.

Liquidated damages for delay

The investigation

The liquidated (i.e. agreed) damages in respect of the investigation are set out in column 1 of the appendix to the tender.

If the investigation is divided into sections, liquidated damages in respect of each section are set out in column 3.

The sums stated need not be the full amount of the employer's foreseeable loss resulting from each week of delay: it can be a lesser sum. The sum can, of course, never be greater than the foreseeable loss.

When the investigation, or a section, is late, the liquidated damages are calculated by multiplying the sum in column 1 (in respect of the investigation) or column 3 (in respect of a section) by the number of weeks of delay. Note that delays of parts of a week are not paid pro rata; three-and-a-half weeks' delay justifies only three weeks' liquidated damages – not three-and-a-half weeks' damages.

When a section has been completed, (whether early, on time, or late) the sum stated in column 1 is to be reduced by the sum stated in column 2 in respect of that section.

If a part of the investigation, not forming a section or a part of a section, is certified as complete, the relevant sum in column 1 is reduced by the proportion that the value of that completed part bears to the value of the investigation.

The same principle applies if part of a section is certified as complete: the sums in columns 2 and 3 are reduced by the proportion that the value of that part bears to the value of the section.

Liquidated damages, site operations

In the appendix to the tender, a separate completion period can be specified for the whole of the site operations. If it is, the whole of the site operations form a section of the investigation (Clause 48(2) (a) (i)). Liquidated damages (or the reduced sum) in respect of delay in completion of the whole of the site operations are to be stated in the appendix.

In the appendix the place provided for this statement is in column 2. This is obviously wrong, because column 2 does not specify the rate of liquidated damages.

One can only assume, therefore, that the figure in column 2 is to be taken as the figure in column 3. Alternatively, from the general structure of the appendix, it may be that these liquidated damages in respect of the whole of the site operations are intended to be in column 1, but nobody remembered to head the column correctly.

When the whole of the site operations are complete, column 1 must be reduced by the relevant sum in column 2. However, there is here no amount stated as to what this sum is, and under the wording of Clause 47 there is no wording for determining the sum.

This part of Clause 47 and the appendix have been so badly drafted as to be unworkable.

Valuing variations

Unless the value of a variation is agreed between the engineer and the contractor, it is to be determined by the following rules.

Rule 1 If the varied work is of similar character and executed under similar conditions to work priced in the bills of quantities it shall be valued at such rates and prices as are applicable.

Rule 2 If Rule 1 does not apply, the rates and prices in the bills are to be used as a basis for valuation, as far as may be reasonable, failing which a fair valuation shall be made.

Rule 3 If the nature or amount of any varied work relative to the nature or amount of the whole or any part of the works renders any rate or price unreasonable or inapplicable, the engineer fixes such other rate as is reasonable and proper.

Rule 4   The engineer can order that any varied work shall be executed on a daywork basis.

If the contractor has received an extension of time in respect of a variation, he is entitled to have the extension valued by having the relevant rule applied to Bill 1 (Preliminaries).

Claims

When the contractor claims for 'cost', this has nothing to do with billed rates. The cost must be proved. Cost includes site costs and overhead costs – Clause 1(5).

    If the contractor intends to claim he must:

1. Give notice to the engineer as soon as reasonably possible after the relevant event – Clause 52(4) (b)
2. Keep contemporary records in support of his claims – Clause 52(4) (b)
3. As soon as is reasonable, submit to the engineer full and detailed particulars of the amount claimed and update it at intervals thereafter.

If these details are not sent in, the contractor deprives himself of entitlement to payment until the claim has been properly substantiated – Clause 52(4) (f).

Quantifying claims

Claims can be justified only from contemporary records – not from memory. Claims should be divided into:

1. *Labour*
   - Prolongation costs – related to the extension of time granted.
   - Disruption costs – the doing of work out of sequence or uneconomically.

   If, however, labour was fully employed elsewhere for eight hours and paid for eight hours, there is no loss. Loss only arises, for example, if labour was employed for five hours but paid for eight hours; or if labour was employed for eight hours and paid for eight hours but the output was only five hours' work.
       This lack of productivity can only be an assessment.
2. *Plant*   Similar principles apply. The period of time paid for is to be compared with the gainful output.
3. *On-costs*   Additional site on-costs need to be justified by records of extra

visits by supervising staff, continued use of equipment, continued security, and so on.

The period of on-costs should be related to the period of extension of time granted, or, in the case of early completion, the contractor's relevant additional period on site.

4. *Invisible losses* Any delay in the completion of the works will delay:

- the payment of the first half of the retention money;
- the second half of the retention money;
- the receipt of money in interims – money that would have been paid in, say, interim 4 gets paid only in interim 6.

The loss resulting from these delays in receipt of moneys is claimed at 2 per cent above the relevant bank rate (Clause 60(6)).

Quantifying overheads

Head office costs cannot be identified individually. They are based on the percentage of the total overhead costs of the contractor – including advertising, research and so on – compared with the contractor's total turnover.

The Hudson formula for calculating loss of head office overheads is:

$$\frac{\text{Head office overheads and profit percentage}}{100} \times \frac{\text{Contract sum} \times \text{Weeks of delay}}{\text{Contract period in weeks}}$$

Settling Disputes

The stages towards an arbitration are:

1. The relevant event
2. Notice of intention to claim
3. The claim
4. Rejection by the engineer of the claim, in whole or in part
5. Challenge by the contractor of the engineer's rejection. This challenge produces a dispute
6. Reference of the dispute to the engineer (Clause 66)
7. Decision in writing by the engineer
8. Reference of decision to arbitration within three months of the decision.

If the engineer does not issue a decision in writing (Stage 7), the reference to arbitration (Stage 8) must be within six months of the reference to the engineer (Stage 6).

The arbitrator has full power to open up, review and revise any decision, opinion, instruction, direction, certificate or valuation of the engineer.

Settling an arbitration

The parties to an arbitration can, at any time, agree terms of settlement. These terms must cover:

- the sum claimed,
- interest on that sum,
- the costs of the arbitration.

If the parties do not agree terms of settlement, one party can make to the other an offer, the terms of which are then sealed and kept from the arbitrator.

If the arbitrator awards more than the amount of the sealed offer, the sealed offer has no effect. If the arbitrator awards less than, or the same amount as, the sealed offer, the party to whom the offer was made should have accepted the sealed offer. That party will then receive the amount in the arbitrator's award; and costs up to the date of the sealed offer, but will be required to pay his own costs and those of the other side from the date of the sealed offer.

Chapter 8

DIFFERENT TYPES OF FOUNDATION

D.J. Sweeney

The viability of a site for development will often depend on the cost of the works beneath the ground surface. In addition to foundation construction, these may involve filling of natural or man-made cavities, ~~construction of a basement or retaining~~ walls, regrading and ground improvement. Unforeseen problems during the groundworks, such as obstructions to piling or excessive groundwater inflow, can lead to extra expense sufficient to threaten the viability of the project. Unsatisfactory performance of the foundations can result in loss or impairment of service or expensive remedial works, and in the extreme, irreparable damage to the structures.

During site feasibility studies it is essential to collect sufficient data to allow reliable conceptual design and costing of groundworks and foundations to be accomplished. In many instances, a thorough desk study (as described in Chapter 6) will yield sufficient information for this purpose. If not, then some ground investigation should be carried out using boreholes and/or trial pits and possibly, geophysical techniques. If carefully planned, it should be possible to carry this out quite inexpensively compared with the liability that could result from an underestimate of the construction costs or distress caused to adjoining property or installations.

This chapter describes some of the more important factors influencing the choice and design of foundations in the UK and attempts to give some insights into design concepts for shallow and deep foundations, excavations for buildings and ground improvement techniques. However, the reader should keep in mind that this is a specialist technical area and expert advice should always be sought.

Factors influencing choice and design of foundations

Ground conditions are encountered in an almost infinite number of forms. They can vary from deep deposits of weak, highly compressible clay, to massive, strong rock at the ground surface; from pits backfilled with industrial waste to limestone with cavernous voids; from clays which shrink or swell following moisture content changes to silts which collapse on wetting; and so on. Loads to be carried by foundations also vary widely from light column loads for retail sheds to enormous loads with high eccentricity from tall buildings; from highly concentrated loads from guyed towers to extensive loads from oil tanks; from variable loads from reciprocating machinery to massive loads from silos.

Frequently it is possible to match sites with loading requirements thereby minimizing foundation engineering problems. Very often there is local foundation engineering 'know-how' that overcomes difficult ground conditions enabling economic foundations to be constructed. However, sometimes economic pressures, such as high land values, will require difficult foundation engineering problems to be resolved, e.g. founding high-rise buildings with deep basements in weak clays or in areas of high groundwater table.

Once feasibility studies are complete and the decision to proceed with a project has been taken, the structural engineers should work closely with the geotechnical engineers to ensure that the optimum foundation solution is obtained. The structure to be supported by the foundations will require certain foundation movement criteria to be met to avoid damage to the structure or its finishes. If it is costly to build unyielding foundations, then the structural engineer may be able to design his structure to accommodate more movement in the foundations. For some structures, virtually no movement of the foundations will be acceptable and this may carry a penalty in the way of high foundation costs.

Whenever difficult ground conditions are involved considerable thought should be given to the project layout so that it fits the site, avoiding, for example, locating the most movement-sensitive structures over the most compressible or variable ground.

In the choice and design of foundations the most basic criteria to be met concern load-carrying capacity and both total and differential permissible settlements. However, there are many other important considerations, such as:

- the possibility of settlements continuing for a long period of time (usually a problem with clay soil),
- the propensity of the foundation soil to shrink or swell due to moisture changes,
- the potential for landslip,
- the possible influence of earthquake loadings or soil liquefaction,

- the threat of a rising groundwater table causing weakening of the soil or flotation of the foundation,
- chemical attack from deleterious materials in the soil or groundwater,
- dragdown on piled foundations due to settlement of weak, surface soils,
- erosion or chemical solution of soil or rock beneath the foundation,
- the possibility of unfavourable influences from activities on adjacent sites,
- noise, vibration and other disturbances associated with certain foundation engineering techniques,
- the influence of past or proposed mining activities.

The choice and design of foundations is undoubtedly a complex subject and often goes wrong. Therefore appropriate expertise should be used in all cases.

Shallow foundations

The term 'shallow foundations' is not a precise one, but is traditionally used in engineering to denote those foundations whose bearing surface is constructed as close to the ground surface as is practicable. The properties of soils, however, determine that such depth may not always be shallow.

Shallow foundations have been used in house and light building construction since the earliest adoption of walls instead of posts as a means of support. The methods used have evolved by tradition and empiricism, in parallel with the type of construction used above ground. In consequence, shallow foundations have rarely been designed in the normal engineering sense; that is by calculation of the loading and its distribution, and the checking of strength and deflection of the soil and structure in response to the loading. As a result failures are still common today.

Type of structure

Before considering the choice of foundation it is necessary to evaluate the performance of the structure under induced ground displacement, and its ability to redistribute load. In the past, large, articulated structures such as cathedrals were built successfully on shallow foundations because the resulting large ground displacements did not alter the structure behaviour and the movements were accommodated in the building fabric without noticeable effect. In contrast recent buildings constructed of lightweight blocks and plasterboard-lined stud walls have cracked unacceptably even with small deflections. An engineer should evaluate the construction form prior to considering the possible type of foundation. At particular risk are:

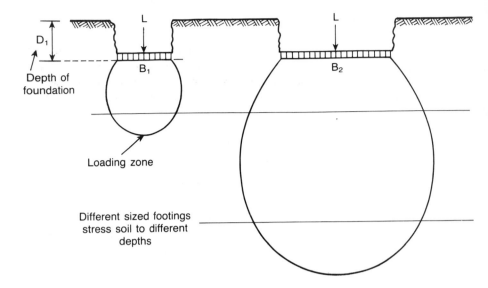

Figure 8.1   *Different sized footings stress soil to different depths.*

- buildings of 'L' or 'T' shape in plan, or with appendages such as porches,
- buildings with large variations of in-plane wall stiffness such as concentrated fenestration adjacent to solid walls,
- asymmetrically loaded buildings with all load being carried by a few walls and other walls unloaded,
- buildings using foamed concrete blockwork as the main structural walling.

Depth of foundations

The depth of foundations will ideally be the minimum that achieves compatibility between the behaviour of the soil under load and the ability of the structure to accept the soil's response. A number of common problems are outlined below.

Consistency of the soil

At shallow depth it is frequently not the case that the soil has consistent properties either in horizontal distribution or with depth. For satisfactory performance, investigations must establish the nature of materials in the full loading zone *below* the maximum proposed depth of foundations – it is not sufficient to have adequate materials simply at the bearing surface. A depth where the increase in effective stress in the soil is less than 5 per cent may be considered a satisfactory exploration depth. The influence of size of footing on depth of stress influence is illustrated in Figure 8.1.

Effect of site levelling

In carrying out a topsoil strip and creating a horizontal terrace for a building in sloping ground, the change in stress due to the soil removal may be more than the weight of the building; the possibility of unacceptable heave occurring as a result of this must be evaluated. At shallow depth on clay soils, buildings of asymmetrical plan form may be at considerable risk.

Sloping ground

Many natural surfaces are not as stable as they appear and depend on natural strengthening effects such as vegetation and partial soil desiccation. The result of site levelling, landscaping, obstruction to the groundwater regime, and making trenches for drainage can induce ground movement which, although not constituting slope failure, does however cause greater displacements than the building can absorb.

Vegetation

Clay soils, and in particular those of high shrinkability, change volume markedly with varying moisture content. Large trees create a desiccation of the soil surrounding the tree to depths of up to five metres. Buildings are thus at risk when adjacent to trees both from continuing desiccation during the life of the tree causing settlement, or from rehydration of the soil after the death of the tree causing heave. The felling of trees before construction requires careful consideration as severe moisture deficits can take at least ten years to return to equilibrium. Unless the foundations are taken below the zone where differential movement may take place, damage is inevitable; in most cases it will be of an unacceptable magnitude because the ground movement is likely to be of the order of 50 millimetres or more. Even when the foundations are at a suitable depth, precautions must be taken to separate the soil zones liable to volume change from interacting with the structure. Heave is a particular problem as the upward movement of the soil is also accompanied by sideways movement creating increased contact pressures.

All the above problems require specialist geotechnical advice if problems are to be avoided. In many cases the cost of foundations may be much greater than normal, and a great deal of attention to detail will be required in the layout of buildings, landscaping and services.

Deep foundations and basements

In many locations chosen for building works the ground conditions at shallow depth will not support the intended structure without excessive settlement occurring. In these circumstances advice must be sought from a specialist geotechnical engineer as to what foundation solution will be appropriate. The possible solutions fall into a number of generic types comprising:

- removal of the unsuitable material and replacement with acceptable fill; this is rarely an economic solution except where large-scale working is possible and/or the unsuitable material is an environmental hazard (i.e. it is contaminated) or contains extensive obstructions;
- as above but with construction of a basement instead of backfilling – by virtue of the increased value of the construction with a basement, the additional costs may be mitigated; this solution is useful for a variety of ground conditions;
- construction of locally deepened foundations to a suitable bearing stratum (piles, piers and caissons);
- improvement of the physical characteristics of the unsuitable material by preconsolidation, dynamic compaction and vibro-compaction methods.

Each of the above will substantially alter the ground conditions, both the soils themselves and the groundwater flow regime. Several of the consequent effects may be damaging to adjacent land or require special attention during construction.

The above-mentioned solutions are further discussed below.

Removal of unsuitable material

The removal of the weight of soil in an excavation changes the *in situ* stress regime in the remaining soil. Where large plan areas are involved the effects may be marked and will vary from rapid expansion and loosening at the surface for materials such as mudstones and siltstones, to longer-term slow heave for clays.

The excavation may also lead to a lowering of the water table and the consequential creation of large hydraulic gradients. For materials such as silts and sands great loss of strength may occur in a quite short time span, resulting in so-called 'running sand' or, more properly, liquefaction. For materials such as gravels the response to the reduction in overburden will be almost immediate and the hydraulic gradients will only lead to groundwater inflow.

The sides of virtually all excavations below the water table will require support at the perimeter except on the rare occasion where the consequences can be ignored.

Basement construction

Two principal matters affect basement construction:

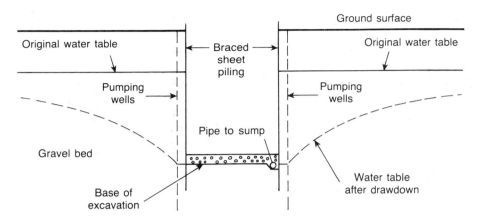

Figure 8.2 *Construction technique for excavating below the water table.*

- the soil reaction inside the excavation area, and
- the effects outside the excavation area.

The weight of a building with a basement is not so great that it is necessarily greater than the weight of soil removed. This is particularly true during construction, but may also be true, unless precautions are taken, for the completed building. In consequence it is necessary for the structural engineer to take account of the full soil and water reactions as the result of removal of the soil from the excavation. Special considerations will be needed to stop flotation during construction and the heave stresses generated by the soil while the concrete is still weak.

The removal of soil not only affects the vertical stress distribution in the soil, but also the lateral stress. For normal construction methods some loss of lateral support is inevitable. By a process of staged construction this may be kept relatively low. The loss of lateral support leads to settlement outside the excavation with consequential damage to adjacent buildings or services. Additional settlement may also occur due to a drawing down of the water table by the excavation. It will be necessary to undertake thorough designs to prevent these effects from being harmful, and to carefully examine the construction methods which are inevitably expensive due to the complex stages of excavation and support needed.

A typical scheme for excavating below the water table is shown in Figure 8.2.

Deepened foundations

The construction of piers or piles gives the opportunity of circumventing most of the characteristics of bad ground. Such systems are not however without attendant difficulties.

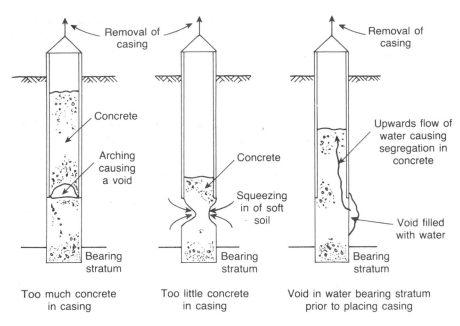

Figure 8.3 *Possible damage to shaft during removal of temporary casing.*

The potentially cheapest method of driving a pre-cast concrete or steel structural member by percussive means has two drawbacks: first the element of noise and vibration and second, limitations on size. Large-capacity piles (over 100 tonnes) are extremely difficult to construct on a building site due to the problems of transport and the size of cranes needed to handle and drive the piles. The noise and vibration caused by driving are normally considered unacceptable in residential or commercial office environments and court injunctions are relatively easily obtained. Ground obstructions may also render driven piles unusable.

A variety of alternative construction methods by drilling or excavating piles and piers exists. These methods eliminate the vibration (though not all the noise) and relatively do not require such large cranes because the piles are created from poured concrete. In consequence large-capacity piles can be constructed suited to tall buildings. Although vibration is eliminated from the pile construction, excavated piles – termed bored cast *in situ* – may suffer problems in their formation either due to difficulties of properly creating the toe or in supporting the sides to prevent collapse during excavation. Some typical problems that can occur are illustrated in Figure 8.3. As in the excavation of basements, the creation of an unsupported hole for the pile may permit a small movement of an adjacent building. The cumulative effect of several piles may be damaging. For this reason the driving of a temporary casing may be necessary. Cast *in situ* piles require good supervision because most of the work is out of sight beneath ground level.

end

Piles or piers are expensive forms of construction due to the specialized machines used and the slow speed of working that is practicable. The specialist geotechnical engineer must have adequate time and information if proper solutions are to be developed.

Ground improvement

This subject is discussed in a later section, but is also mentioned here because piles that are driven may be used to displace and thus preconsolidate the otherwise unsuitable ground. By a combination of consolidation of the ground and the load-carrying capacity of the piles, a composite material is created which may satisfactorily carry the design load. Such methods are not very flexible in use, but for simple building shapes on relatively uniform materials they may be useful.

Rafts and piled rafts

Raft foundations have a variety of applications. They are useful for building on soils of low bearing capacity and are the most practicable solution where structural columns or other loaded areas are so close to each other that individual pad foundations would almost touch. Raft foundations are particularly useful in reducing differential settlement on variable soils or where there is a wide variation in loading between adjacent columns or other applied loads.

For carrying smaller structures, rafts may take the form of a plain slab or a slab reinforced with cross-beams. For larger structures, cellular rafts may be used, which achieve stiffness while minimizing the amount of concrete required.

Rafts have several specialist applications. For example, they may be effectively used to cope with mining subsidence, allowing a subsidence wave to pass beneath without damage to the supported structure; or to form 'compensated foundations' where the ground is excavated to some depth and replaced with an equivalent weight of building with settlement thereby minimized.

The design of raft foundations is not straightforward as the stresses that will occur in a raft are strongly dependent on the relative stiffness of the raft and the supporting ground. Various types of contact pressure distribution that can occur are shown in Figure 8.4.

Where very heavy structures are to be carried, it may be necessary to

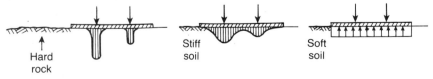

Figure 8.4 *Typical contact pressure under raft foundations.*

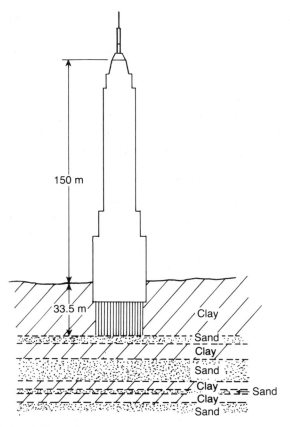

Figure 8.5   *Piled raft foundation.*

consider use of a piled raft. Again, the design of such structures is not straightforward and it is common to assume that all loading is carried on the piles without any transmission of load directly from the raft to the ground. This is usually conservative and design methods that address the true behaviour of piled rafts are likely to be cost-effective. If piles are over-designed, with great vertical stiffness, they will tend to carry all the load with the raft transmitting virtually no load directly to the ground. Where appropriate, modern design practice is to underdesign the piles, thereby allowing the ground beneath the raft to make a significant contribution to carrying the load resulting in design economies. A piled raft solution is illustrated in Figure 8.5.

Ground improvement

The load-bearing capacity of poor or weak ground, whether natural or fill, can usually be improved by using ground engineering techniques. Broadly these fall into two groups:

- shallow soil stabilization which consists of treating a superficial layer or layers of soil, and
- deep ground treatment comprising the improvement of ground in depth (deep soil treatment).

Shallow soil stabilization

The simplest form of improving a soil is to make it more dense using compaction plant, usually some form of roller appropriate to the type of soil. The most effective compaction will be achieved if the soil is at or close to its optimum moisture content and if compaction can be carried out on thin layers of soil.

Some poor quality soils may be made usable or strengthened by the addition of lime or cement, normally in the range of 2 per cent to 8 per cent of the dry weight of soil. These additives are mixed intimately with the soil, usually in place, by rotavating equipment and the mixture is then compacted. In particular, wet, clayey fills can be made usable by adding lime to reduce their plasticity and to improve their strength; cement added to granular non-plastic or low plasticity soils can form sub-bases for roads or even pavements such as estate roads or car parks for light vehicles. Suitably stabilized granular soils can carry relatively heavy structures such as medium or even high-rise buildings.

Deep ground treatment

Deep ground treatment is usually carried out where loose and/or poor quality low-strength materials are present to considerable depths. Treated ground is usually suitable to carry low-rise buildings, warehousing, light industrial units, storage areas and tanks, and housing. It should be noted that the treatment of waste materials and particularly urban refuse is problematical. Refuse should be some 30 years old or more; otherwise it may still settle over many years as undecomposed organic matter continues to break down.

The most common methods of deep ground treatment are described below.

Recompaction in layers

Where the unsuitable ground is less than two or three metres thick and above the water table, material can be excavated and replaced in layers, 150 to 250 millimetres thick, each layer being rolled to an adequate density.

Preconsolidation by surcharging

Compressible soils such as weak organic alluvial clays, loose sands and silts, and waste materials can be improved by preloading. The principle is to cause settlement in advance of construction by loading temporarily with material to an equivalent, or even greater loading than will be imposed by the permanent structure. The consolidation rate of clays can be very slow, in which case

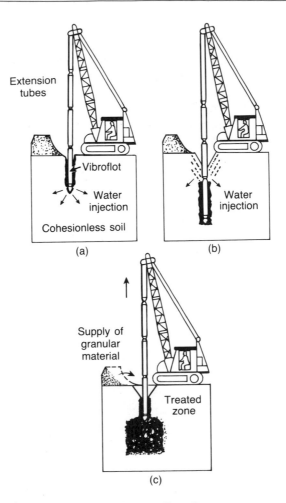

Figure 8.6   *Vibro-compaction using a vibro-flot.*

vertical drains can be installed to accelerate the process by shortening the drainage path for water being forced out of the soil.

Vibro-compaction

Vibro-compaction is used in the deep compaction of cohesionless soils. A vibro-flot (a large vibrating probe) is lowered into the ground; the vibrations cause the soil particles to pack closer together giving an increased soil density and thus causing a depression at the surface which is filled with imported granular fill. The vibro-flot inserts are made on a grid pattern. After such treatment relatively high loads may be accepted. The process is illustrated in Figure 8.6.

Vibro-replacement (stone columns)

A frequently used technique for improving made ground, poor quality clay fills and soft natural clays is vibro-replacement. As with vibro-compaction, a vibro-flot is lowered into the ground where it forms a hole. The hole is then gradually filled with stone which is compacted in place by regular reinsertion of the vibro-flot to form stone columns. Usually clay fill should have been in place for at least ten years before application of this technique. Spacing of stone columns is typically in the range of 1.5 to 3.5 metres. The closer spacing would be used for clusters of stone columns beneath pad footings whereas the wider spacing would be appropriate under floor slabs. Depths of stone columns typically vary between about two and six metres and may exceptionally extend up to about nine metres. A compacted granular blanket is placed over the stone columns to distribute stresses from the supported structures.

Dynamic compaction

Dynamic compaction is a heavy tamping method applied mostly to granular fills and natural loose sands, though in some cases it can be employed for finer grained soils, and clay backfills above the water table, to improve their mechanical properties. The site is initially covered with about a metre thickness of granular fill. Heavy weights (concrete or steel plate blocks) of some eight to twenty tonnes are dropped from heights of 15 to 40 metres several times on a grid pattern with repeated coverage at certain intervals of time depending on the ground conditions. For treatment depths down to ten metres conventional craneage may be used but for greater depths specialized equipment is needed. The method requires some 20 to 50 metres' separation from existing structures according to their state and ground conditions. In urban areas the noise and vibration may cause a nuisance and the public may require protection against flying debris.

Grouting

Grouting is a process of injecting into the ground, usually under pressure, liquid grouts (with or without fillers) which penetrate voids and displace existing fluids and which then set to give strength. Chemical grouts are used for small pore spaces as in sands. The large voids of old sewers and mine workings can be grouted using various mixtures of cement, sand, gravel and Pulverized Flue Ash.

Chapter 9

REDEVELOPMENT OF CONTAMINATED LAND

D.L. Barry*

The scale of redevelopment on contaminated land has been closely correlated with a number of factors, principally the restriction on urban expansion and the decline or relocation of many large-scale industrial operations. Thus, the scarcity of greenfield sites and the commercially advantageous locations of many former industrial sites, combine to highlight a new phenomenon, namely the hazards to new sensitive land uses arising from the legacy of chemical spillages and waste disposal activities, for example. During the 1980s there was extensive re-use of such sites and a considerable, but not always adequate, body of advice was published by the Department of the Environment and other bodies such as BSI, CIRIA, and professional institutions. The most extensive range of advice has been, effectively, from the DoE which has produced guidance notes on a range of specific and general contaminated sites.[1-7]

Much debate has taken place on the range of issues involved, with a particular benchmark being reached with the publication of the House of Commons Select Committee Report on Contaminated Land in January 1990.[8] The implications of that report could, if the recommendations are followed, be very considerable in both technical and legal terms, not least of these, perhaps, being the particularly pertinent question of *caveat emptor* or 'let the buyer beware'. That issue, however, is also being addressed by the Law Commission.

* The author is grateful to his colleagues, particularly Ms A.K. Feeney, for their help in preparing this chapter.

In the following sections, an outline is given of the policy relating to the redevelopment of contaminated sites, the types and relevance of hazards, the manner in which these should be investigated and assessed, and options for rehabilitation. This chapter should not be seen as an adequate basis for addressing the issues in detail, and due reference must be made to more explicit information sources. Moreover, many of the sites in question require very considerable experience and expertise, involving a number of disciplines, including chemistry, environmental health and geotechnical engineering, for example.

The redevelopment of contaminated land sites also invariably presents physical hazards that need to be overcome. Physical hazards can be in the form of underground tanks, chambers and other obstructions. On some sites the physical instability of the groundmass is such that ground stabilization measures will be necessary before redevelopment.

Redevelopment policy

The concern about contaminated sites is not confined to redevelopment hazards since, in some instances, the wider environment can be at risk, e.g. groundwater pollution from the leaching of chemicals. Developers considering the purchase of a contaminated site for redevelopment should consider such potential implications since the ownership of such land may carry with it responsibilities relating to off-site effects.

There has also been considerable debate regarding the objectives in clearing contaminated sites. Should those objectives relate only to the immediate proposed use? This has been the basis of official policy in the UK so far, but it has come under criticism from those countries who believe that the condition of land should always be such that any use is possible. The House of Commons Committee[8] accepted that to decontaminate a site to make it suitable for virtually any future use is not justifiable. Instead, provided the question of migrating pollution, whether liquid or gaseous, is properly addressed, the site can be cleaned to suit the immediate use. This will not always require a complete once and for all decontamination of the site. It is essential, however, to recognize that where contaminants remain on site after redevelopment, there must be an effective record made of the original and as-built ground conditions. Otherwise, future redevelopers of the site may fall into the on-going trap of assuming that clean 'current' uses are synonymous with clean histories.

Prospective purchasers and developers should be aware of the planning and other implications of redeveloping contaminated land. Broadly, the approach which should be followed is set out in Department of the Environment Circular 21/87[1] and ICRCL Note 59/83.[2] In essence, it is the developer's responsibility to:

- satisfy himself that the site in question is suitable for the intended use, or can be made suitable if it is not already so;
- demonstrate to the satisfaction of the relevant local planning authority that the proposals take adequate account of contamination or any other environmental constraints when applying for planning approval for the proposed development;

and, if such approval is granted,

- accept and retain responsibility for the continuing safety and secure occupancy of the completed development.

All these are important matters which will require careful consideration by prospective developers. Adequate time should be allowed for this. It is then the responsibility of the local planning authority to decide whether to approve the development application. This is done using the procedures set out in the planning legislation contained in the various Town and Country Planning Acts. Once planning approval has been obtained and the development is being designed, attention to the requirements of building control legislation is needed. Here the Building Regulations 1985, in particular Approved Document C,[9] should be followed for advice.

Types of contaminated land

The main source of contaminated land is usually land that has been formerly used for industry, mining or waste disposal. A number of site types can be identified, which almost invariably present redevelopment hazards:

- waste disposal sites
- land close to waste disposal sites
- gasworks
- chemical works
- munitions works
- metal mines, smelters, foundries
- asbestos works
- tanneries
- paper and printing works
- railway land
- oil refineries
- scrapyards
- sewage works.

However, it would be wrong to assume that only large sites present significant hazards; for example, a dental laboratory could have gross mercury contamination, or a timber yard wood preservative hazards.

Chemical contamination of sites may arise through industrial processes, accidental spillages and leaks, storage of raw and waste materials or from fugitive emissions from the industrial plant itself. Direct contamination of land can also occur through disposal of contaminated wastes. Another major environmental hazard on waste disposal sites is that presented by the gas generated from the biodegradation of the waste materials. (Such sites can also present profound physical difficulties. It is probably fair to say that former landfill sites present a disproportionate scale of potential risks due to the extensive gas migration potential when the local groundmass is highly permeable or fissured, for example.

Chemical hazards can be in the form of liquids, solids and gases, each of which represent fundamental conflicts with the proposed or possible use of a site.

Relevance of hazards

Ground contamination can be relevant in the following principal ways and have consequences for a range of targets.

Nature of hazard	*Targets*
Toxicity – inhalation	Site investigation workers
– ingestion	Construction workers
– skin contact	Building materials and services
Corrosiveness	Future site users
Phytotoxicity	Plant life
Carcinogenicity	Water regime
Combustibility	
Explosiveness/flammability	
Pathogenicity	
Radioactivity	

The relevance of some of these hazards can vary greatly with proposed site use, which can range from a relatively insensitive use such as a surface car park to a highly sensitive one such as an allotment area. Thus, for example, where sites are being considered principally for industrial redevelopment, phytotoxicity to plant life could be irrelevant for the greater part of the site.

The types of contaminants that might be encountered are:

- toxic metals, such as cadmium, lead, arsenic, nickel and zinc
- aggressive substances such as acids, sulphates, chlorides, sulphides, acids

- oily and tarry substances such as phenols
- flammable gases such as methane
- asphyxiant gases such as carbon dioxide
- combustible substances such as coal and coke dust
- asbestos
- volatile organics
- pathogenic substances.

Many sites contain a number of these contaminants and it is not uncommon to have to design solutions to cover several hazards. Equally, a remedy for one problem can exacerbate another.

Investigation strategies

General

Knowledge of the ground conditions and contaminants may well require the collection of samples from boreholes or trial pits for analysis but investigating a site is not simply a matter of digging holes. Without some idea of where to put the holes and what to look for, sampling and analysis could well be a waste of time and money. Very valuable information can be gained simply from a review of historical information on the site and its general environs, and a site visit. Clearly, judgements from such surveys will need corroboration as a project proceeds, as with conventional ground investigation strategies.

Developers proposing to acquire land for future use are well advised to commission a pre-purchase survey of their sites. In many ways, pre-purchase surveys are likely to be the most cost-effective of all. *Prima facie* evidence of contamination from site history information can significantly influence the value of the land. Such information can sometimes be gained in as little as a few hours' archive research but normally it takes a few days to establish a suitably comprehensive profile of the history and specific nature of former uses of a site. Time spent on establishing the site history could well save money later on when detailed sampling and analyses are needed. Moreover, such information is critical to interpreting the range of conditions that can be encountered.

The fact that a site might currently appear innocuous can be totally misleading; a temporary surface car park on a former gas-works site can mask very significant pollution. Similarly, knowledge that land was previously used for, say, ship-breaking will more or less guarantee that there is extensive asbestos on the site.

BSI have produced a draft code of practice relating to the identification and investigation of contaminated land.[10] Particular attention should be paid to the advice in that document and any surveys commissioned should be based on its recommendations, making use of experienced investigation consultants wherever possible.

Historical information

Historical information on a site will give an indication of the likely types of contaminants present, and may also suggest the potential scale of this contamination. Information which is particularly relevant includes:

- past uses, owners or occupiers;
- the type and location of processes, raw materials, products, waste residues and methods of disposal;
- the site layout above and below ground at each stage of the development;
- mining history, including shafts and roadways;
- the presence of waste disposal tips, abandoned pits and quarries;
- information on geology and hydrogeology.

Useful sources of historical information are:

- maps – Ordnance Survey (current and historical), geological survey maps and former work plans
- photographs – aerial and ground
- statutory authorities – local planning and environmental health departments, waste disposal authorities, National Rivers Authority, British Gas, British Coal, etc.

An extensive list of historical sources is given in the earlier mentioned BS1 Draft Code of Practice.[10]

Preliminary site visit

The historical information collected should be supplemented and clarified by a preliminary site visit. Attention should be paid to the surface topography and site layout, both of which can provide useful indications of the type of contaminants likely to be present. The presence of phytotoxic substances may be indicated by the absence of poor vegetation growth. Waste materials such as slag, ashes, asbestos, scrap metal and industrial or chemical waste may be present on the ground surface. Their presence could require immediate action to remove or abate the hazards they pose.

Any drums and containers that litter the site should be treated with special care as they may contain hazardous substances. Due note should be made of unusual odours or emissions of fumes from the ground surface, as these may signify the presence of chemical waste residues. Likewise, smoke, charring or smouldering indicate underground combustion, either current or in the past. Where underground combustion has taken place, the ground might be very unstable. The general topography of the groundmass may also indicate areas of infill, which can be checked against the historical information.

Ground investigations: location of sampling points

The historical information usually forms the basis for designing the ground investigation. It is preferable that sampling points are not solely located on grid patterns, as to do so might ignore clear visual or historical evidence. However, the number of sampling points must be sufficient to identify areas of intense contamination, the general distribution of contamination across the site and its variation with depth. The ICRCL recommends that 'the spacing of sampling points should, in principle, be no larger than the largest area of contamination that could be handled without difficulty, if it were not found during the investigation, but only discovered during development'. For example, on a large former gasworks site,[3] typically this would represent grid intervals of 50 or 100 metres, and on a smaller site closer spacing of 10 or 25 metres. A good general approach is to plan on the basis of a roughly geometric grid over the whole site area, with extra sampling points in areas where historical or visual evidence indicates potential contamination.

Conventional techniques such as trial pits and boreholes are generally the most effective means of collecting samples for chemical testing. For some purposes trial pits have many advantages over boreholes but in practice it is usual to require both since the contamination survey should be integrated, as far as possible, with the ground engineering or geotechnical investigation which normally requires boreholes. The visual evidence from trial pits is invaluable in assessing the scale and nature of contamination. On some sites, for example on landfill sites where the depth of waste is likely to be greater, a number of boreholes will have to be drilled to determine both the full extent of the wastes and the underlying geology. Remote sensing techniques, e.g. geophysical methods, may provide useful additional evidence but they do not usually yield sufficiently specific information to enable a reliable assessment of contamination to be made.

Samples are best taken from specific strata rather than at fixed depths. It is prudent to take extra samples during the fieldwork and then make an appropriate selection of such samples for analysis. In this way a reasonable range of strata across the site is represented adequately. Groundwater samples should be collected from all excavations in which water is encountered. Also, it should be ensured that sufficient solids and liquids are collected for subsequent analysis.

The usefulness of colour photographs of the site in general and the excavated pits in particular, cannot be stressed enough. Too many investigations fail to include these records, which together with properly compiled borehole and trial pit logs, are essential to effective interpretation.

Chemical analysis

Chemical analysis is relatively expensive and so it is important that the results obtained are relevant to the needs. For example, phytotoxicity is unimportant in some contexts and testing for heavy metals might be a waste of resources. On the other hand, it can be false economy to be overly restrictive in testing since a lack of data can compromise subsequent decision making. It is important to keep in mind that where materials are to be disposed off site, the waste disposal authority will require data for classification purposes. Also on sites where large volumes of groundwater are likely to be disposed of during rehabilitation, data on the level of contamination of the groundwater will be required by the NRA prior to disposal to a sewer or a river body. A more critical need for such data could, of course, relate to off-site and downward migration and the consequences therefrom.

For each site the range of contaminants, the variations in their concentrations and the scale of hazard will be different. In specifying chemical testing due account should be taken of the potential contaminants identified by the historical and site observations as well as the proposed use. As indicated earlier, the ICRCL has produced a series of advisory notes on the redevelopment of specific types of contaminated sites, namely, landfill sites, sewage works and farms, scrapyards and similar sites, sites contaminated with asbestos, and gasworks.[3–7] These can be used for further guidance on the type of contaminants that are likely to be encountered and the hazards which they present.

Landfill gas investigations

Gas surveys require a somewhat different approach to chemical surveys, because gas regimes are much more dynamic and may change with time. Where sites are being examined for gas, particularly landfill gases, special sampling techniques are needed. In effect a perforated probe is installed into an excavated pit or borehole and these can be subsequently monitored for gas concentrations with portable instruments. In the case of landfill gas it is critical that due consideration is given to carbon dioxide as well as methane. Also, too often no attempt is made to measure volumes of gas; without this information it is not meaningful to assess the hazards. Another investigation technique involves 'spiking' the ground surface with a metal probe. However, where this is used to assess the gas regime, extreme care must be taken not to interpret low concentrations of methane as being of no consequence, since there are many variables which can affect gas readings. These include low permeability ground, either by virtue of site cover materials or ground saturation following rainfall.

The Department of the Environment technical memorandum on the monitoring and control of landfill gas (Waste management Paper 27)[11] provides guidance on a number of gas-related issues and is particularly relevant to redevelopment proposals adjacent to operational or restored landfills. Advice on techniques for measuring gas emissions from contaminated land is given in a technical report produced by the Building Research Establishment.[12]

Assessment of conditions

While good quality data are essential to proper assessment, it is all too easy to try to assess conditions solely on the results of analysis and to ignore the physical conditions actually encountered in the site investigation. The assessment process is complex, requiring considerable experience and does not simply involve a comparison of chemical analysis data with published guidelines. As indicated earlier, actual conditions or, more correctly, hazards are not always defined by analysis data. The physical forms of contamination, contexts, scales, depths and interfaces with the proposed development are all critically relevant, as are the potentials for migration of both ground contamination and gases.

In this regard, the role of the water regime is particularly important. Groundwater movement can greatly influence the relevance of contamination; for example, a cover system with a capillary break layer can be rendered ineffective if the site becomes inundated by water. (Such break layers are designed principally to prevent upward migration of soluble compounds through the action of capillary forces.)

The ICRCL has produced concentration guidelines for a range of contaminants above which it is considered appropriate to either take a more rigorous interest in the conditions (i.e. 'threshold values'), or take action to reduce the scale of hazards (i.e. 'action levels'). There is often confusion in the application of these guidelines on the part of regulatory authorities who wrongly interpret the 'threshold values' as maximum permissible values rather than levels below which there is no relevant hazard. It is akin to confusing acceptable with desirable.

In any assessment of ground contamination where durability of building materials is of concern, reference should be made to the Building Research Establishment guidance notes on the protection required for concrete exposed to soil and groundwater with high sulphate levels[13] and CIRIA Report 98 'Material Durability In Aggressive Ground'.[14]

Health and safety

The range of hazards that can be present during the development of contaminated sites can be very wide, and precautions need to be taken to protect workers engaged either in investigation or construction activities. It is the responsibility of the designers and developers to highlight within contract documents the need for appropriate measures to safeguard workers' health and they should incorporate the general provisions of the Health and Safety at Work Act 1974.

The hazards can be reduced if suitable safety precautions are taken. For the site investigation worker, in particular, the requirements for protective clothing such as chemical protection suits can be identified from the historical survey and preliminary site survey which can highlight the majority of hazards. The information gained from the site investigation can likewise be used to identify the hazards to the construction workers. In all site investigation and construction work, good standards of personal hygiene should be ensured, such as thoroughly washing hands before smoking or handling food. Also, prior to any site work being carried out, the presence of live electrical cables, water and gas supplies should be identified from statutory service and local authority records.

Showers can be an advantage on construction sites, where workers are dealing with contaminated materials. This allows effective dousing of an individual to be carried out if the need should arise. To prevent contamination of eating and other areas, strict codes of practice should be introduced; for example, soiled protective clothing and boots should be removed before entering these areas.

For both site investigation and construction work, it is important to use intrinsically safe tools where the presence of flammable gases is suspected. In confined spaces, comprehensive gas monitoring should be undertaken and if breathing apparatus is required, advice should be sought.

The need for a full-time safety officer on the construction site will depend on the scale and nature of risks involved. In defining this need consideration should be taken of:

- the known or suspected hazards;
- the risks of hazards arising;
- the duration of the works or periods during which the hazards are most likely to occur.

The safety officer's remit should include:

- ensuring that the site workers are made aware of the types of hazards and degrees of risks associated with them;
- regularly sampling and analysing the working conditions;
- advising on the appropriate handling or treatment of chemical substances encountered;
- instructing on protective clothing and safety apparatus to be used;
- organizing and supervising any permit-to-work system.

Guidance notes are published by the Health and Safety Executive that are particularly relevant on contaminated land sites.[15–17]

Rehabilitation options   *effects on construction – need to set violat it.*

Several options are available for the treatment of contaminated ground. The choice will obviously depend on the level of contamination, distribution of the contaminants, the proposed end use of the site, the scientific and technical limitations of the options available, and the temporal and financial implications of the proposed treatment options.

The principal methods currently used to deal with contamination are:

- excavation of the contaminated soil or materials and either disposal off site in a suitably licensed waste disposal site or in a controlled manner on the site itself;
- treatment of the material to remove, detoxify or immobilize (to reduce their 'availability') the contaminants, either on site or at some other suitable location;
- encapsulation of the contaminants;
- 'dilution' of contaminated material with clean fill to reduce the concentrations of contaminants.

Excavation

Removal of contaminated material for off-site disposal does usually eliminate the problem as far as the development site itself is concerned, but there are disadvantages. These include:

- the hazard and nuisance created for the rehabilitation workers and the neighbourhood, including the odour and noise impact arising during waste removal and backfilling operations;
- the availability of suitably licensed disposal sites to receive the waste and, if large volumes of material are involved, the high cost of removal; and
- disposal of contaminated groundwater that may arise during works.

Furthermore the problem has not really been solved, only moved to another place.

On some sites this option might not provide a satisfactory solution, particularly if the contamination extends beyond the boundaries of the development site or if contaminants have already migrated into the groundwater that underlies the site. On landfill sites in particular, following the removal of the waste from the area of development, some protection measures may have to be installed to prevent gas and leachate migration into the site from other areas.

Encapsulation/covering

Contaminants may be isolated from the proposed development by covering the site with either capping or buffer layers. The implications of this system include the physical problem of raising site levels, the possible upward migration of mobile contaminants and maintaining the integrity of the system in face of subsequent developments. Also, for such systems to work effectively, a high standard of workmanship must be adopted during their installation. For this option, building foundations and services may also require protection by ground cut-off techniques, buffer zones (e.g. clean backfill) or applied coatings.

Treatment

There are a number of potential benefits to be gained from the treatment of soil through detoxification or immobilization of the contaminants. To date this practice has received relatively little attention in the UK, largely because of the cost disadvantage relative to either removal or covering. However, in the future this may change, particularly in the light of the House of Commons Report.[8] That report highlighted the fact that current practices in the UK for treatment of contaminated land paid too little attention to groundwater protection, and in most cases rehabilitation options did not reduce the level of contamination and/or just involved transferral of the contamination to another site.

Treatment options for contaminated soil include:

- physical – separation or extraction of contaminants;
- thermal – removal of contaminants by evaporation or heat destruction of contaminants;
- chemical – hydrolysis, oxidation for electrolysis of contaminants in soil resulting in detoxification;
- microbial – innoculation of soil with microbes that are capable of degrading contaminants to inert substances;
- stabilization/solidification – physical or chemical reduction of hazardous nature of soil (but does not actually remove contaminants from soil).

Before treatment of any contaminated soils, it is most cost-effective to separate the waste according to the degree of contamination. Obviously if the level of contamination in some areas is below the technical limits of the process to be used, there is little point in treating the material. A good site investigation, i.e. appropriate sampling distribution and chemical analysis, will indicate the level of contamination and identify areas of low and high contamination.

Dilution

Where the concentrations of contaminants are not excessive and the volumes of material involved are not large, it may be possible to achieve satisfactory conditions by mixing the contaminated materials with clean fill so as to reduce the overall contamination levels on the site. Such a course of action does, however, require detailed knowledge of the concentrations present and how they vary across the site and with depth. Adequate space on site is also needed for segregating the contaminated material, mixing it with the clean fill in the required proportions and then stockpiling it for re-spreading on the areas from which it came before development takes place.

Post-development responsibilities

DoE Circular 21/87 points out that when development takes place on a contaminated site it is the developer's responsibility to ensure the continuing safety and secure occupancy of the site. This will in most cases require some form of regular monitoring of the completed development to check that the remedial action taken before development continues to provide adequate protection against any hazards.

Where contamination has not been eliminated before redevelopment, it is important that suitable records of the original and as-built conditions are kept. The long-term monitoring requirement is not easily defined: the local authority will have an on-going interest and 'duty of care' under its public health and general environmental powers, though if as a result of such information it becomes apparent that some action is needed to correct post-development problems, the responsibility to carry out the necessary work would rest with the developer.

Notes

1. Department of the Environment and the Welsh Office. DoE Circular 21/87 (Welsh Office 22/87), Development of Contaminated Land. HMSO, London, 1987.
2. ICRCL Paper 59/83 Interdepartmental Committee on the Redevelopment of Contaminated Land. Guidance on the Assessment and Redevelopment of Contaminated Land, 2nd edition, July 1987, DoE.
3. ICRCL 18/79 Interdepartmental Committee on the Redevelopment of Contaminated Land, notes on the Redevelopment of Gas Works Sites, 5th edition, April 1986.

4. ICRCL 17/78 Interdepartmental Committee on the Redevelopment of Contaminated Land, notes on the Redevelopment of Landfill Sites, 7th edition, May 1988.
5. ICRCL 23/79 Interdepartmental Committee on the Redevelopment of Contaminated Land, notes on the Redevelopment of Sewage Works and Farms, 2nd edition, November 1983.
6. ICRCL 42/80 Interdepartmental Committee on the Redevelopment of Contaminated Land, notes on the Redevelopment of Scrap Yards and Similar Sites, 2nd edition, October 1983.
7. ICRCL 64/85 Interdepartmental Committee on the Redevelopment of Contaminated Land. Asbestos on Contaminated Sites, 1st edition, May 1985.
8. House of Commons (Session 1989–90) 170–1, Environment Committee First Report on Contaminated Land, HMSO, London.
9. Building Regulations 1985: Approved Document C. Site Preparation and Resistance to Moisture, HMSO, London.
10. British Standards Institution (1988), DD175:1988 Draft for Development, Code of Practice for the Identification of Potentially Contaminated Land and its Investigation.
11. HMIP (1989), Waste Management Paper No. 27 The Control of Landfill Gas. A Technical Memorandum on the Monitoring and Control of Landfill Gas, HMSO, London.
12. Crowhurst, D, (1987), *Measurement of Gas Emissions from Contaminated land*. Building Research Establishment, DoE.
13. British Standards Institution (1985), Structural Use of Concrete Part 1. Code of Practice for Design and Construction.
14. Barry, D.L. (1983) *Material Durability in Aggressive Ground*. CIRIA Report 98.
15. Health and Safety Executive (1985), Guidance Note EH40: Occupational Exposure Limits, HMSO, London.
16. Health and Safety Executive (1984) Guidance Note EH10: Asbestos Control Limits Measurement of Airborne Dust Concentrations and the Assessment of Control Measures, HMSO, London.
17. Health and Safety Executive (1984) Guidance Note EH42: Monitoring Strategies for Toxic Substances, HMSO, London.

Bibliography

Cairney, T. (ed.) (1987), *Reclaiming Contaminated Land*, Blackie & Son, London.
CIRIA (in press), *Building on derelict land*.
DoE (1987), *Problems arising from the redevelopment of Gas Works and Similar Sites*, April.
ICE (in press), *Recycling Derelict Land*.
Smith, M.A. (ed.) (1985), *Contaminated Land: Reclamation and Treatment*, NATO: CCMS Plenum N.Y.

Plate 9.1   Trial pits can show clear evidence of a succession of strata. (W.S. Atkins 1990)

Plate 9.2   No reasonable site investigation will prove all deposits; here an unexpected encounter with phosphorus (W. S. Atkins 1990)

Plate 9.3   The legacy of contamination on some sites is obvious (W. S. Atkins 1990)

Plate 9.4   This site has extensive deposits of (buried) asbestos from ship-breaking (W. S. Atkins 1990)

Plate 9.5   Careless demolition can exacerbate problems, in this case contamination from PCBs (from the transformer) (W. S. Atkins 1990)

Chapter 10

H.M. LAND REGISTRY

P.J. Smith

H.M. Land Registry is a government department which has been in existence since 1862. Its function is to provide a safe, simple and economic system of land transfer in England and Wales. Registration of title to land in Scotland and Northern Ireland is dealt with by entirely separate organizations. The system was first established to ensure that the interests of individual or corporate bodies owning land or legal interests in land are protected. For this reason, the information held by the Registry is at present not open to public inspection, although under enabling legislation recently enacted, inspection of the register and certain related documents by members of the public is to be permitted after a date to be set in late 1990 or thereabouts.

About 11 500 staff are employed by the Land Registry, and they are located in 18 district land registries distributed across England and Wales, and at a headquarters office in London.

The main body of legislation which governs the operations of the Land Registry is the Land Registration Act 1925 and the Land Registration Rules 1925 made under that Act. Unless otherwise stated they are the Act and Rules referred to elsewhere in this chapter. Under existing legislation, land does not become registered until it is sold, or granted on long lease within a designated area of compulsory registration. For this reason, the pattern of registration is spasmodic, and indeed under present legislation, a property which is not bought or sold will never actually get registered at all. Nevertheless in areas where compulsory registration has been in operation for a long period, more than 98 per cent of the land may be registered. About 13 million titles are registered at the present time, and this figure is increasing by about .66 million titles per annum. It is estimated that the total number of registered titles could rise to about 22 million in the long term given appropriate changes in the statutory provisions relating to compulsory registration. It should be noted that all areas of England and Wales will be subject to compulsory registration of title on sale by the end of 1990.

The official records

The primary official records created and maintained by the Land Registry are the register, the filed plan and the public index map. For each registered title there is held a register in the form of a card or cards, identified by a unique title number, which provides an official description of the land, the name of the owner, and details of any legal interests which adversely affect the land, such as mortgages, restrictive covenants, easements etc. Once registered, the title to the land is guaranteed by the state.

Under modern practice, every registered title has its own official filed plan, which shows the extent of land registered under the particular title number, and which serves to support the official description of the land in the register. The Registry also maintains a series of about 400 000 maps and map extracts which together constitute the public index map. On the public index map is shown the position, extent and title number of every registered title. Filed plans and index maps are based on large-scale Ordnance Survey maps.

The extent of land registered under each title is shown on filed plans and index maps by a red edging. On the public index map, each registered parcel is annotated with its title number, although in urban areas, a parcel number is usually shown on the face of the index map, which refers to an associated parcels index, where the title number and other information associated with the parcel may be found. On the filed plan, a range of coloured shadings, edgings, hatchings, measurements and other annotations may be found, which together provide further information on the boundaries of land registered, or are the means of reference to specific entries on the register, usually relating to restrictive covenants, easements and so on.

Searching the records

It is perhaps a little surprising that until the end of 1990, when the provisions of the Land Registration Act 1988 are brought into force, it has normally not been possible for members of the public to search the records held by the Land Registry in order to determine the ownership of land and the various legal interests which may affect it. This is not to say that searching facilities have not existed, but they have been generally available only to those persons or corporate bodies who have been given specific authorization to make an inspection. Thus a potential purchaser of registered land may be provided with a written authorization from the landowner to inspect the filed plan and register of the relevant title, and to obtain office copies from the Land Registry. Similarly, certain bodies may be authorized by statute to inspect the register, with or without the permission of the registered landowner, usually in connection with matters relating to aspects of law enforcement. The exception is the public index map record, which has always been open to public inspection, but which provides very limited information.

This situation has been a source of frustration and practical difficulty for property developers and those responsible for assembling sites for development. Difficulties have also arisen with regard to determining the position of boundaries of development sites, when it has not been possible to identify adjoining landowners to discuss and settle uncertainties regarding the position of common boundaries. Towards the end of 1990, on a precise date yet to be fixed, the situation will change, and anyone will be able to search the register and filed plan records held by the Land Registry, and order copies thereof. These searching and copying services will be provided by the Land Registry on payment of fees, which may be varied from time to time. Although it will be possible to inspect the public index map, register and filed plan records by personal attendance at the district land registry serving the area within which the relevant land is situated, applications for an official search of the records may be made by post on prescribed forms and on payment of the appropriate fees. Searching by post has been by far the most common method of searching hitherto, and this is likely to continue. It should be noted that unless it is known that the land concerned is registered, and its title number is known, it is usually necessary first to make a search of the public index map to obtain this information, before a search of the register and filed plan can be made, or copies provided. If the land is not registered, and no application for registration is pending in the registry, the Land Registry will of course be unable to provide any information on ownership or related legal interests.

Where a search of the register is intended to lead to an application for registration, it will be possible (as hitherto) to apply for a search which reserves priority for the subsequent application for a period of 30 working days.

Interpretation of map records

Unlike unregistered conveyancing, a definitive plan is prepared for every title. It is not 'for the purpose of identification only'. Each register describes the land in the title as 'the freehold/leasehold land shown and edged with red on the plan filed at the Registry . . .'.

Plans prepared by the Land Registry are based on the Ordnance Survey map. Rule 272 states that 'the Ordnance Map shall be the basis of all registered descriptions of land'.

The public index map consists of a series of large-scale Ordnance Survey maps or map extracts covering the whole of England and Wales. In urban areas the map scale is 1/1250. In rural areas it is 1/2500 scale, and 1/10 560 or 1/10 000 scale in mountain or moorland areas.

The various scales of Ordnance Survey maps used as the basis of H.M. Land Registry's official map records have specified accuracy tolerances, and these must be taken into account when interpreting them.

Filed plans are generally produced at the same scales as above, but may be produced at larger scales, or have inset plans at larger scales, to show complex detail as necessary. Almost all filed plans are prepared subject to the provisions of Rule 278 of the Land Registration Rules, known as the 'general boundaries rule', which reads as follows:

278.(1) Except in cases in which it is noted in the Property Register that the boundaries have been fixed, the filed plan or General Map shall be deemed to indicate the general boundaries only.

(2) In such cases the exact line of the boundary will be left undetermined – as, for instance, whether it includes a hedge or wall and ditch, or runs along the centre of a wall or fence, or its inner or outer face, or how far it runs within or beyond it; or whether or not the land registered includes the whole or any portion of an adjoining road or stream.

(3) When a general boundary only is desired to be entered in the register, notice to the owners of the adjoining lands need not be given.

(4) This rule shall apply notwithstanding that a part or the whole of a ditch, wall, fence, road, stream, or other boundary is expressly included in or excluded from the title or that it forms the whole of the land comprised in the title.

The 'general boundaries rule' (Rule 278, Land Registration Rules 1925) is a practical and economical alternative to the 'fixed boundaries' approach first prescribed under the Land Registry Act 1862. Despite the terminology used in Rule 278, it is the modern practice to prepare filed plans to as great a degree of accuracy as is allowed by the deeds lodged, and the accuracy of the Ordnance Survey map. Where a boundary is not defined by physical features, the general boundaries rule still applies.

The commonly known legal presumptions relating to property boundaries may still be applied to 'general boundaries' in registered conveyancing. Declarations as to boundaries entered on the register may serve to rebut such presumptions.

Exact boundaries can generally be established only by inspection and agreement with neighbours on ownership of boundary features and the relationship of these features to the legal boundaries.

Under Rule 276 there is provision for registration with fixed boundaries, although such cases are extremely rare. A filed plan of a title registered with fixed boundaries will show the precise position of the legal boundary in relation to adjoining physical features. Sufficient co-ordinated points are shown on the filed plan to enable the boundary to be reinstated in its correct position in relation to the national grid survey network.

A registered boundary cannot be fixed without the agreement of the adjoining owner, except by direction of the Court.

It is often possible to satisfy the requirements of a landowner by arranging for a declaration by the relevant parties as to the ownership of the physical feature marking a boundary to be entered in the property register.

A boundary fixed under Rules 276 and 277 may still be varied at a later date if any encroachment by adjoining owners is for a period and of a nature which would constitute adverse possession. The fixing of a boundary does not afford any special protection, in this respect.

There are obvious difficulties in preparing official filed plans of properties which include only part of a building at a certain floor level or levels. In the most straightforward case, where the entirety of a floor within a building is to be registered (together with land outside the building) the building is tinted (usually in blue), and the property register may be drafted to describe the situation thus:

26A Acacia Avenue, Pembury

Note: As to the part tinted blue on the filed plan, only the first floor flat is included in the title.

Sometimes a property includes different extents at several floor levels. In this situation, the extent at each floor level may be plotted on to the filed plan, and the resulting areas are numbered. Notes to the property register are then drafted to indicate the floor levels affected within each area numbered.

Where the extents on different floors are unusually complex, and the plan to the lease is of the quality produced by an architect or building surveyor, the whole of the site of the main building may be edged red on the filed plan and the property register is then drafted to refer to the land in the lease.

Anyone who is concerned with the selection of sites for development should pay particular attention to the following points when considering the extent of land shown on the filed plan of a registered title. First, unless one is attending a land registry to make a personal inspection, it is unlikely that the document being inspected is the original filed plan. If it is a plan bound into a land certificate or charge certificate, it will be a true-to-scale copy of the plan filed in the Land Registry, but care should be taken to check the date when the copy filed plan and register contained in the certificate were last lodged at the Land Registry and brought up to date. It is just possible that a new filed plan has been prepared and filed in the registry, based on the latest revision of the Ordnance Survey map, which will show up-to-date detail of the physical boundaries and other features on the site. The last application date shown in the entries on the copy of the register indicate the relevant governing date.

When inspecting an official copy filed plan, particular attention should be paid to any areas which are tinted, edged or hatched in green. These areas are not included in the title. Areas edged in green will be found to be labelled with a Land Registry title number, and this indicates that the area of land in question has been transferred out of the title of the land edged red to the new title number shown, and registered under different ownership.

Registration of developing estates

Two aspects of registration need to be considered here. First, the requirements for plans and description when applying for first registration of the development site (if not already registered); and second, the requirements for plans and the special procedures recommended in connection with the registration of sales of plots or other forms of subdivision.

An application for first registration must include sufficient particulars by plan or otherwise, to enable the land to be fully identified on the Ordnance Survey map (Rule 20 (iii)).

Some 15 per cent of applications for first registration are found to have shortcomings relating to plans or descriptions.

In the case of well established property, a verbal description may sometimes be sufficient, but an accompanying plan is preferred, and is essential in the case of registration of land for development.

Where plans are supplied with an application to the registry, defects in plans are found to exist as follows:

Plans outdated or inaccurate	5% of total intake
Minor omissions, errors or inaccuracies in plans	3% of total intake

Defects of this nature often require surveys by or on behalf of the Land Registry to check the position on site, and usually require requisitions to be raised to correct the plans. In a further 7 per cent of cases, staff may exercise discretion in accepting the plans without further requisitions, even though they contain some inaccuracy or other defect. The aim is to register an extent of land which accords with the apparent intentions of the parties.

In the case of subdivisions of registered land, under Rule 79, applications for registration must be accompanied by a plan showing the land being dealt with, unless it is clearly defined on the vendor's filed plan (which is hardly ever the case on developing estates). However before transfers of plots from the estate are processed, consideration should be given at the earliest possible stage to the use of the system of approval of estate layout plans.

Full details of the procedures for approval by the Land Registry of estate layout plans of registered building estate are contained in the Registry's Practice Leaflet No. 7. The purpose of seeking approval of an estate layout plan by the Registry is to enable any material discrepancy between the registered estate boundaries and the external boundaries of the proposed development to be resolved before negotiations for the sale of plots commence. Following approval, applications for certificates of inspection of the filed plan and for official searches of the register can be made by reference to the plot number(s) shown on the approved estate plan, and the cost of providing separate plans is avoided.

The Royal Institution of Chartered Surveyors has co-operated with the Land Registry in the production of Practice Leaflet No. 14, which is primarily aimed at surveyors and engineers concerned with the layout of estate development. The leaflet specifies the accuracy standards required for estate plans for approval, and recommends procedures which will ensure that changes in layout are effectively monitored on site, and that the Land Registry is advised of the changes.

The most common reasons for the rejection by the Land Registry of estate plans lodged for approval are as follows:

1. Material discrepancies exist between the external boundaries of the proposed layout and the registered title boundaries
2. The precise extent of each plot is not clearly indicated, or is not identified with a unique reference number
3. Insufficient details are shown on the layout plan to enable it to be related to the filed plan.

The problem which most frequently arises after approval of an estate plan, is that development does not take place in accordance with the proposed layout. Often this becomes apparent to the Registry only when it commissions a survey of the estate to update its maps to enable the mapping of transfers of plots to be completed.

An approach adopted by some of the larger developers which minimizes the possibility of problems of layout changes is to base the plan lodged for approval on a survey of the actual site layout after erection of the building has begun. As long as the subsequent erection of fences around the plots is closely controlled, there is little possibility of any significant departures from the proposed layout occurring.

Boundary disputes

Because of the operation of the general boundaries rule, the register will not normally provide information on the ownership of physical features which enclose registered land, unless there happens to be a declaration noted on the register, or if, exceptionally, a registration is with fixed boundaries.

The Land Registry will not enter into discussion or correspondence concerning disputes over boundaries unless they concern registered land. Where a dispute occurs, and is drawn to the attention of the Land Registry, the department will generally endeavour to assist in resolving the dispute so far as it can.

A common example of where the Registry may assist is if there is a dispute as to which physical features on the ground are shown as registered boundaries on the filed plan. The registry may be able to assist by attendance at a site meeting, possibly to carry out a survey. The department also has access to early editions of the Ordnance Survey map, and in some cases detailed survey reports and air photographs, all of which may help to resolve a problem.

Where a physical boundary has been removed, and the parties seek assistance, the Registry may assist in relocating the position of the boundary, within the limits of accuracy of the Ordnance Survey map on which the filed plan is based.

The services described are provided free to the parties who request them, but it is to be emphasized that the advice given is entirely impartial, and the department will always seek to ensure that all the parties concerned are fully aware of any investigations which are undertaken.

Issues which need to be taken into account in assessing the merits of the case of each party when considering and advising on boundary disputes affecting registered land are:

- The operation of the general boundaries rule
- The accuracy of the Ordnance Survey map
- The operation of legal presumptions, and the possibility of them being rebutted by other evidence
- The effect of adverse possession
- The significance of plans, verbal descriptions and dimensions in plans and deeds in registered and unregistered conveyancing
- Proprietary estoppel, where for example, a landowner may have acquiesced in an encroachment by a neighbour, and in subsequent expenditure in improving the affected land
- The possible existence of past agreements relating to the position of boundaries.

This list is not exhaustive.

It has to be said that where a dispute centres on the ownership of boundary features or the land on which the features stand, and consideration of these issues does not assist the parties, or reference of the matter to court for judgement, it is recommended that the latter course is avoided, if at all possible.

In a number of cases, enquiries or disputes are referred to the Land Registry, and as a result of investigations it may be found that the register or filed plan is in some way in error, and should be rectified. The statutory provisions for rectification are contained in section 82 of the Act. The grounds for rectification are very widely drawn, and it is not possible to enter into detail in this book. The register or the filed plan may be rectified by an order of the Chief Land Registrar or an order of the Court. The wide grounds for rectification are reduced by the principle contained in sub-section (3) that the register will not normally be rectified against an innocent registered proprietor who is in possession. This means, for example, that where a double conveyance took place before registration, and the second purchaser was first registered, and occupied the land, rectification would not normally be carried through, even if it transpired that the 'first purchaser' is in a position to claim a better title, provided it is within the limitation period.

Under section 83 of the Act, where a person suffers loss following rectification or because of the failure of an application for rectification, that person is *prima facie* entitled to financial compensation (i.e. indemnity). In the example above, it may mean that the Land Registry will pay compensation even though a problem has arisen which is no fault of its own (i.e. applications for registrations have to be dealt with on a 'first come, first served' basis). No indemnity is payable where an applicant has caused or substantially contributed to the loss by fraud or lack of proper care.

Lastly, it should be noted that the Chief Land Registrar has certain judicial powers, and may conduct formal hearings in order to adjudicate on questions arising on applications for registration and for rectification, but not on claims for compensation or loss, although in practice he may and often does settle claims by securing agreement.

The future

The continuing growth in home ownership and the number of titles registered, together with the advent of public access to the register, will mean further increases in the workload handled by the Land Registry. Demand for its services will be further fuelled by the growing interest in the development of an integrated national land or geographical information system, of which the datasets held by the Registry are perceived to constitute essential components.

To improve service and efficiency the Land Registry is currently implementing a programme of computerization of its register records system. The system is currently installed at three land registries, and will be extended to all registries by 1994.

In the case of the map records, since 1983 feasibility studies have been conducted relating to the use of digital mapping technology for land registration purposes. Following the acquisition of a graphics system and extensive development of application software, a production system was installed at the Peterborough Land Registry in 1986, and was recently further extended at that office. A further system will be installed in the Plymouth district Land Registry early in 1991. There are proposals for extension of the digital mapping system to further offices.

It may be of interest to consider to what extent the developments by the Land Registry are consistent with the requirements of a possible future integrated land information system. The main features may be summarized as follows:

1. The map records are based on the Ordnance Survey map, which is generally accepted as the framework to which all map based land information systems in the UK should be referenced
2. It is essentially a land parcel based system, with a record of ownership and related legal interests attached to each parcel
3. The UPRN (unique property reference number) is the Land Registry title number, but graphical data can also be accessed through postal address or post code, or simply the nearest street or road name. The system is capable of being developed to enable data to be retrieved by use of a different UPRN of a parcel, if a universal system of numbering ever came to be agreed as a standard
4. Spatial searching can also be carried out by reference to National Grid coordinate values
5. Access from the map to the attribute (text) data, and vice versa, may be gained through the title number, although the hardware and communications linkage to enable this to be achieved has not yet been configured
6. The Land Registry graphics and text records are designed to be simple and easy to interpret.

Computerization of the Land Registry's map and text records is being implemented primarily to fulfil the requirements of owners of registered land and related interests, and the members of the various professional bodies and institutions who provide the range of services which enable property transactions to take place. Nevertheless, the developments in progress are consistent with those which need to be taken to enable the Land Registry's property records to be accessed through an integrated property information network, if one is established in the long term.

When things go wrong

Defects in plans and descriptions in deeds can give rise to a great deal of practical difficulty and expense not only to the parties involved, but also to the Land Registry when applications for registration are received. The Land Registry examines the plans and descriptions very carefully to determine the extent of land which should be registered, and its investigations will usually reveal discrepancies between plans and descriptions, or discrepancies between the plans and descriptions and the physical situation on the site. When this occurs, it can often mean that the registration cannot proceed to completion until the problem identified has been resolved. This can be a cause of trouble, expense and embarrassment to property developers, landowners and the solicitors dealing with the conveyancing aspects of the transaction.

On very rare occasions, the defects may go unnoticed by the Registry's plans staff, and the registration may proceed to completion. As a result, land may be registered with an extent which does not accord with the beliefs or intentions of one or other of the parties, and sometimes of both parties. The latter situation is often the most easily resolved, because if both parties can agree on their true intentions, the Registry can usually provide a simple means of documenting an agreement which can then be put into effect by rectification of the relevant filed plans and registers as appropriate.

The following cases serve to illustrate some of the most common problems encountered in the plans and descriptions for land for development. They also illustrate that the Registry is prepared to assist, and in some cases to compensate landowners for actual loss, in circumstances defined in the relevant sections of the Land Registration Act 1925. The cases illustrate difficulties arising from inaccurate plans, plans drawn to too small a scale for their purpose, and the inaccurate setting out of new development. The cases described are real, but names of places and persons are not revealed, to preserve confidentiality.

Case A

Builder X acquired a piece of land for development with a curved boundary on its southeastern side which was intended to follow the line of a new estate road. Another builder Y acquired land adjoining to the southeast of the curved line. The estate road was built slightly to the northwest of its intended position, and as a result, part of X's land fell to the southeast of the road line. Both X and Y proceeded to erect residential development on each side of the roadway. Y erroneously extended his plot boundaries to the frontage of the roadway over the strip of land in the ownership of X. The developed plots were sold, and the Land Registry granted title to the new plot owners up to the road line, in accordance with the transfer plans prepared by Y. When the error was discovered, it was necessary to rectify X's title to exclude the land conveyed to the owners of plots sold out of X's estate. The Land Registry paid compensation to X for the loss of his land, as well as the costs of the valuers and solicitors involved.

Comment

The origin of the difficulties was in the setting out of a curved roadline, which did not accord with the builder's conveyance plans. In this case, the Land Registry erroneously accepted the roadline as the correct position, and in consequence had to pay the costs of resolving the problem. However if the error had been discovered by the Land Registry, as is more usually the case, the parties would normally have to negotiate and settle the matter before registration is allowed to proceed. This can be time-consuming and expensive. Errors in curved boundaries are often difficult to detect. It is advisable to employ a competent land surveyor to ensure that they are set out correctly.

Case B

An estate developer prepared an estate layout plan at 1/500 scale. He lodged a copy reduced to 1/1250 scale with the Land Registry, for its approval in connection with the issue of searches and certificates of inspection in respect of the sales of the plots shown on the plan. The reduction in scale made the plan difficult to interpret in areas of fine detail, but nevertheless the plan was approved by the Registry. As a result of certain ambiguities in the extents of plots 103 and 104 on the estate plan, the sale of plot 104 took place, and was registered to include part of a parking space subsequently found to be intended to be included in the sale of plot 103. A transfer to the purchaser of plot 103 also included the part of the parking space, but was excluded from the title to plot 103 as it had already been registered under the title to plot 104. Prior searches, in respect of both plots, made by reference to the small-scale estate plan did not bring the discrepancy to light, and it was only discovered after the transfer of plot 103 was received for registration. It was only after very lengthy correspondence and negotiation that the purchaser of plot 104 could be persuaded to give up the piece of parking space. The filed plans of plots 103 and 104 were rectified, and the Land Registry paid compensation to the owner of plot 104, together with solicitors' costs.

Comment

The origin of the problem was a double conveyance by the developer which was not detected by the Land Registry as the result of its approval and use of too small-scale an estate plan. This error by the Land Registry is unlikely to be repeated due to changes in its practices. Where a double conveyance of this nature occurs in the future, it is likely to be the developer who will have to deal with the protracted and expensive negotiation before sales of the plots are accepted for registration. Estate plans lodged for approval and the plans contained in transfer documents must be accurately drawn, unambiguous and to a sufficiently large scale to show fine detail.

Case C

A conveyance of part of an area of farm land contained a poorly drawn 1/2500 scale plan showing the land conveyed, with a long and undefined curved boundary on its northern side. Land to the north was retained by the vendor as farm land for cultivation. The description in the conveyance included a statement of the area of land conveyed. When an application was lodged for registration at the Land Registry, it was accompanied by a proposed estate layout plan drawn to 1/500 scale which the applicant stated had been approved by the vendor, although it had not been signed by him, neither was it referred to in the conveyance. The quoted area in the description in the conveyance was checked with that shown on the small-scale deed plan, and found to be in reasonable accord, although the curved boundary caused some difficulties in precise calculation. The large-scale layout plan said to have been approved by the vendor was approved for official search purposes. The land was later developed and the plots sold off, including 12 plots which adjoined the curved northern boundary of the estate. In less than a year of the development and sale of the plots, the original vendor complained that the plots occupied part of the land which he had retained. A precise check of the area of land covered by the development showed that it did indeed exceed the stated area in the conveyance by 0.42 acres. The Land Registry subsequently paid compensation to the farmer for the loss of the land, plus interest and costs.

Comment

This is a further example of the problems which can be associated with the inaccurate setting out of undefined curved boundaries. The small-scale conveyance plan limited the chances of detecting any discrepancy between the plan and the stated acreage, particularly as the excess land was distributed in the form of a narrow crescent-shaped strip along the northern boundary. In this case the description, which included a statement of area, was taken to prevail over the plan.

Chapter 11

WHAT HAPPENS WHEN THINGS GO WRONG

N.M. White

A case history

At 6.30am on the morning of 9 April 1983 a tower crane being used to construct an office block at Wilson Street, Grantley, collapsed without warning. Serious damage was caused to the contract works as well as to plant and equipment belonging to the main contractor and to various sub-contractors. A self-employed electrician who was just arriving for work suffered leg injuries, and damage was caused to the roof of a neighbouring cottage belonging to Miss Mary Blenkinsop. As the firemen were clearing away debris they discovered Miss Blenkinsop's cat, Felix, bleeding and concussed. The progress of the works was seriously interrupted for three months.

Winds at the time of the accident were gusting to 75mph, but the jib had been left free to weather vane and the crane had been designed to withstand substantially stronger wind speeds. A full investigation was therefore called for.

Before considering the conclusions of the investigation and how the responsibilities of the various parties were resolved, the legal and insurance considerations will have to be examined.

Legal and contractual liabilities

The developer has an overall responsibility for damage suffered by third parties. This arises largely in nuisance which is a tort arising out of the duties owed towards occupiers of neighbouring properties. Nuisance normally arises from a dangerous state of affairs rather than an isolated incident. For example if a structure collapses because it was in a dangerous condition this may give rise to an action in nuisance, but if the collapse is due to an isolated incident of negligence it will not. The essential difference between negligence and nuisance is that an employer is not normally liable to third parties for the negligence of his independent contractors, but it is not so easy for him to avoid blame in cases of nuisance.

Liability may also attach to an employer under the rule of Rylands *v. Fletcher* which confers strict liability for loss and damage arising from the escape from land of dangerous things brought on to that land. It is for the Courts to decide what are or are not dangerous things in this context, but the rule has been held to apply for example to sparks generated by a fire on a building site, as well as to chemicals, and in certain instances to non-domestic water. The rule of Rylands *v. Fletcher* is regarded by some as being a branch of the law of nuisance. As in the case of nuisance it is not an adequate defence to demonstrate that the damage was caused by the action of an independent contractor.

The architect

The architect will have a wide-ranging professional responsibility actionable in negligence for design, choice of site, recommending builders, suitability of materials, compliance with bye laws, and supervision. The standard of care required to be exercised by a professional man is that which ought reasonably to be exercised by a qualified person in that profession. This goes beyond the standard of care required of people not acting in a professional capacity.

Engineers

Engineers who design the foundations and calculate structural loads have responsibilities to ensure that the ground conditions are suitable, that the foundations are properly designed and constructed, that loads imposed upon each component are properly calculated, and that suitable materials and workmanship are employed.

Liability extends not only to the architect's or engineer's contractual partner, but to any person he ought to have had in contemplation at the time of the act in question, including for example persons who later occupy the building. However, the rules are not hard and fast, and questions of proximity and scope of legal duty take up a great deal of time in the Courts.

The main contractor

The main contractor is generally required to indemnify the employer under conditions of contract. He also has a wide-ranging liability in negligence.

Under the Occupiers' Liability Act 1957 he has a responsibility in respect of injury to persons visiting the site. Under the Health and Safety at Work Act 1974 he assumes various responsibilities including duties arising from provisions relating to breach of Building Regulations. The Building Act 1984 includes further provisions relating to breach of Building Regulations. The Defective Premises Act 1972 requires work on the construction of dwellings to be carried out in a workmanlike way with proper materials, making them fit for habitation when completed. The NHBC scheme requires a builder to offer a guarantee to a house purchaser. And if that were not enough, there are implied conditions in building contracts requiring that a contractor shall carry out the work in a proper and workmanlike manner and that materials shall be fit for the intended purpose. The implied conditions are often reinforced with specific warranties.

All in all, building contractors have onerous and far-reaching responsibilities arising out of the work they perform. The potential scope of a contractor's liability has been somewhat reduced by the House of Lords decision in D & F Estates *v*. Church Commissioners for England (1988) where it was ruled that in the absence of personal injuries or damage to other property caused by defective work (plaster in that case) claims for repairs to the defective work represented pure economic loss for which the contractor owed no duty of care to subsequent occupiers.

Sub-contractors

Sub-contractors have similar responsibilities to those of main contractors, but only for their respective parts of the works. They will normally be required to provide an indemnity to the main contractor in respect of any liabilities devolving upon the main contractor due to the sub-contract works.

Local authorities

Local authorities are required to pass plans and ensure that Building Regulations are enforced. This requires inspection of the works at various stages to ensure compliance. Local authorities have been the butt of a long line of legal actions resulting from the failure to ensure adequacy of foundations. Their liability often arises in tandem with the contractor, but they can on occasions be an easier target for example if it is suspected that a contractor might not be able to satisfy a judgement. Their duties arise under the Public Health Act 1936 and the current bye laws, and were refined by the House of Lords in Anns *v*. Merton London Borough Council (1978) as well as a number of subsequent cases.

Suppliers

Suppliers attract liability to their contractual partners under the Sale of Goods Act 1980 which stipulates that goods must be of merchantable quality and fit for the purpose. Liability also arises in negligence. The famous 'snail in the ginger beer bottle' case of Donaghue *v.* Stevenson decided by the House of Lords in 1932 still allows those who have suffered harm to sue suppliers in negligence. The scope of suppliers' liability has recently been extended by the Consumer Protection Act 1987 which gives effect to the European Product Liability Directive of 1985. This allows a wide range of parties, who need not be contractual partners, or even consumers for that matter, to sue suppliers for harm caused by defects in products without proof of negligence.

It is possible to restrict liability between contractual partners by inserting exemption clauses in contracts, but the validity of such clauses has to pass the test of the Unfair Contract Terms Act 1977. It is not possible to contract out of liability for personal injury at all, nor, when dealing with consumers, from the duty to supply goods of merchantable quality and fit for the purpose. In general, exemption clauses must be reasonable, and it is for the Courts, applying the logic of the man on the Clapham Omnibus, to determine what is or is not reasonable. Important criteria when deciding upon whether a clause is reasonable are the relative sizes of the parties and their familiarity with the type of clause involved.

Responsibility for property on site

As a general rule each party bringing materials on to a site is responsible for those materials unless conditions of contract specify different treatment. Contractors are required by their employers to complete the works, and the occurrence of loss or damage is generally speaking no excuse for not carrying on. Most contracts do in fact include insurance clauses to ensure that contractors do not experience financial embarrassment as a result of complying with these obligations.

Indemnity clauses

It is normal for construction contracts to contain indemnity clauses whereby the contractor is required to indemnify the employer in respect of third party loss and damage arising out of the carrying out of the works. Under JCT Conditions the contractor is required to indemnify the employer against loss and damage arising from negligence. This responsibility is effectively extended to include non-negligent liability to occupiers of neighbouring properties caused by collapse, subsidence, heave, vibration, weakening of support or lowering of ground water, under Clause 21.2.1. of the JCT 1980 Conditions. By the terms of this clause, the contractor is required to take out insurance in the joint names of the contractor and employer to cover legal liability for such loss and damage.

Under ICE Civil Engineering Conditions, and FIDIC Conditions which apply to a range of overseas contracts, the contractor is required to indemnify the employer in respect of all losses and claims arising out of the execution of the works regardless of negligence. This is subject to a proviso in respect of losses which are the unavoidable result of the execution of the works in accordance with the contract. Precisely when dust or vibration is unavoidable can prove extremely difficult to resolve since neither the Courts nor the Institution of Civil Engineers have provided any guidance. Such matters have to be negotiated objectively between the parties working on site, bearing in mind that failure to reach agreement can lead to delays in compensating innocent third parties.

Latent Damage Act

It is beyond the scope of this chapter to give detailed consideration to the statutes of limitation. It is however worth considering briefly the implications of the Latent Damage Act 1986. This Act, which interrelates closely with the Limitation Act 1980, lays down that an action for damage to property becomes time-barred either six years from when the damage actually occurred, or three years from the date of knowledge, whichever is the later, but in no event more than 15 years from the breach of duty. An exception is where there has been deliberate concealment of a defect in which case time does not start to run until the defect is discovered or should with reasonable diligence have been discovered. The 15-year long-stop is of some comfort to designers who might otherwise continue to incur liability for past misdeeds well into their dotage.

Insurance

One way or another loss and damage is likely to find its way to one or more of the insurers covering the parties involved. Whilst most parties would not need to be persuaded to take out insurance, there are some situations in which insurance is compulsory, for example:

- Road Traffic Act 1988
- Employers' Liability Compulsory Insurance Act 1969
- By insurance clauses in building contracts
- Professional advisers may be required to provide evidence of pro-fessional indemnity cover before their services are retained.

The main insurance policies likely to be involved are set out below.

Contractors all risks (CAR)

This type of policy, which may cover the client as well as the contractor (and sometimes sub-contractors), insures the works and materials against 'all risks'. This convenient term does not mean that insurers pay for all conceivable types of loss or damage. The types of loss and damage which are normally not recoverable are:

1. Damage caused deliberately or wilfully by the insured party seeking to recover
2. Foreseeable or inevitable damage
3. Damage normally recoverable under motor, marine or aviation policies
4. Cash, which is normally insured under a separate policy
5. Penalties and consequential losses due to delays. Delay or advanced profits cover is sometimes made available on major projects
6. Wear, tear and gradual deterioration
7. Damage occurring after handover
8. War, radiation and sonic bang
9. Shortages discovered at stocktaking
10. The policy excess – normally applying separately to each occurrence
11. Defective workmanship, material and design.

Numerous variations of the defective workmanship, material and design exclusion exist. Even the most restrictive clauses normally allow claims for damage caused by the defect to other insured property. The wider clauses will also pay for the cost of gaining access to the defective part, and occasionally even for the cost of replacing the defective part itself, subject only to the exclusion of the proportion of such cost which relates to betterment. Identifying the cost of the defective part, and relating that to the policy cover can be a mind-bending task, particularly when the same wording is used for such diverse risks as buildings, civil engineering works and machinery. To determine the cost of the defective part in for example a slipped motorway embankment, a seized gas turbine, or a collapsed hotel ceiling can be exceedingly complex and it is often necessary to consider not only the literal wording, but also the intentions of the parties.

Contractor's public liability insurance

This may be linked to the CAR policy, but will in any event form a separate section subject to its own terms and conditions. The policy covers legal liability for damage to property and personal injury. Exclusions are likely to relate to:

1. Risks normally covered by an employers' liability policy
2. Risks normally covered by a motor policy
3. Property belonging to the insured, but if two or more parties are covered by the same policy a cross liability clause will allow one party to recover against another as though separate policies were issued to each

4.   Liability for products supplied
5.   Liability for defective design
6.   War and radiation risks
7.   The policy excess – for property damage only.

Plant and equipment insurance

Although major items of plant and equipment will often be specified and covered under a separate plant policy, insurers frequently cover contractors' plant along with works and materials under the 'Contractors all risks policy' without any requirement to provide specific details. This is to allow for the fact that numerous items of plant are utilized on a contract site, many of which are hired in for short periods under conditions of hire which require the contractor to accept responsibility for loss and damage. The contractor also requires cover in respect of tools and equipment, site huts and their contents. It is also normal for contractors to insure their employees' personal effects subject to individual limits.

Products liability insurance

Cover normally applies to liability for personal injury and damage to property resulting from defects in products. Cover normally excludes the cost of the product itself as well as damage more usually covered under general liability policies.

Professional indemnity insurance

Although it is comparatively rare for claims against design professionals to succeed, the potential liability arising from a trivial error can be enormous, and unless designers have adequate cover a claim can render them bankrupt. The cost of cover increases with the limit of liability and professionals need to consider carefully their maximum exposure when choosing how much insurance to buy.

Relatively few insurers engage in this specialist business. Even though claims may be few in number, high levels of payments have resulted in professional indemnity premiums becoming significant items of expenditure.

All policies relate to 'claims made' against the insured during the policy period regardless of when the act of negligence occurred, or indeed when the third party suffered injury or damage. This gives rise to the need for a stringent declaration at renewal. Confessing to knowledge of an incident in a renewal declaration when a claim has not actually been made against him should not lead to the policyholder being penalized. With a 15-year long-stop provision under the Latent Damage Act, it will usually be necessary to keep up cover after retirement. For members of established partnerships this is no hardship, but those in business on their own may have to make special provision for future liabilities.

How matters are resolved

The great majority of cases of loss and damage are the subject of insurance claims, and it is therefore normal for insurance companies to control investigations and negotiations.

Most large contractors have their own insurance departments, and those personnel will normally be actively involved, especially on major claims, to ensure that claims are handled correctly, and that provision is made for proper assessment and recovery of both insured and uninsured losses. It is usual for insurances to be arranged through specialist broking firms who ensure not only that claims are collected from insurers, but also that their clients obtain full and fair settlement in accordance with the terms of the policies.

Most insurance companies employ their own claims inspectors, but it is normal for large-scale property damage losses to be handled by loss adjusters. Engineers or other experts may be appointed either by insurers or loss adjusters to investigate causation. Solicitors tend only to become involved when litigation is pending. The approach to handling of professional indemnity claims varies between insurers, some of whom instruct solicitors from the outset, while others prefer to appoint loss adjusters in the early stages.

Case history – concluded

The site agent in Grantley was a busy man when he arrived on site. One of his first telephone calls was to his insurance manager. The claim was duly notified to the contractors all risks and public liability insurers and they nominated loss adjusters to represent their interests. To make matters simple, a project policy covered the joint interests of the developer, the main contractor and the sub-contractors against all risks of loss or damage to contract works, plant, and materials as well as public liability.

The works were repaired by the contractor and his sub-contractors, and the costs which were recorded on daywork sheets were checked by the adjuster who applied the conditions of the policy, including the policy excess of £5000, before agreeing settlement and taking signature to a form of acceptance. The agreed sum was then paid by the insurers. No insurance provision was however made for the very substantial costs arising from the three-month delay. The cost of the delay was calculated by the insured's quantity surveyors and passed to the loss adjuster to be added to the subrogation claim against the parties responsible for the accident.

The crane which belonged to a sub-contractor was a total loss and was replaced at their insurers' expense subject to deductions for wear and tear and salvage.

Miss Blenkinsop asked the contractors what they proposed doing about her roof, and they advised her to report the matter to her household building insurers. She was however shocked to learn that the impact peril under her buildings policy only covered damage caused by vehicles, animals, aircraft and trees – not tower cranes. She then got her nephew to write to the developer – who passed the letter to the main contractor under the indemnity clause in the contract. The main contractor passed it to the tower crane sub-contractor, who sent it to the consulting engineer, who sent it back to the developer. After living for two months with a tarpaulin over her roof, Miss Blenkinsop then lost patience and placed her claim in the hands of solicitors. The solicitor concluded that liability attached to the developer, the main contractor, the crane sub-contractor, the crane manufacturer, the consulting engineer, and Grantley District Council, and threatened to issue proceedings against them all. A site meeting was then convened and it was agreed that the main contractor would repair the roof and that the project public liability policy would meet the cost subject to pursuing recovery. Details were checked by the loss adjuster and the claim was settled subject to deduction of a further excess of £2500.

The injured electrician was off work for several weeks and presented a claim against the main contractor through solicitors. Settlement was negotiated by the claims inspector of the public liability insurers, no excess being applicable in this instance.

Consulting engineers appointed by the CAR insurers established that defective slew ring bolts had been supplied by the crane manufacturers, and it was deemed unlikely that the crane would have collapsed if proper materials had been fitted. It was also determined that one of the piles beneath the base of the tower crane passed through an isolated layer of peat which caused negative skin friction and therefore reduced the bearing capacity of the pile. It was shown that if more boreholes had been taken prior to driving the piles this danger would have been identified. This was determined to be a contributory cause of the collapse, and the CAR insurers decided to pursue recovery against both the crane manufacturers and the engineer who designed the piles. They decided however that there was insufficient evidence to involve the local authority.

The crane manufacturer and the engineer reported claims to their products liability and professional indemnity insurers respectively who each appointed solicitors to act on their behalf. Both sets of solicitors maintained firm denials of liability on the grounds that the accident had been caused by storm, by another party, or by circumstances outside their clients' control. Writs were issued, followed by statements of claim, defences, requests for further and better particulars etc., and documents were duly exchanged.

Nothing would however persuade any of the parties to change their stances, and six years after the crane collapsed, an assortment of 34 barristers, solicitors, engineers, insurers, loss adjusters and contractors arrived at the High Court. Although the case was only due to start at 11am, the barristers representing the contractors' all risks insurers, the crane owners' insurers and the engineers' insurers were there at an early hour and were seen huddled together in a corner of the corridor. With 20 minutes to go before the start of the case, they broke off to confer with their instructing principals, and then reconvened. At just two minutes to 11am a message was sent to the judge informing him that the parties had agreed settlement and that his services would not be required.

The three parties agreed to pay one-third each, which was greeted with beaming smiles and hearty handshakes. The contractors' insurance manager, who had suggested a three-way split three years previously, discovered that the barrister's briefing fee was almost as much as his annual salary. He was seen disappearing in the direction of the nearest pub muttering obscenities.

Last but not least, Felix made a rapid recovery and was soon back with Miss Blenkinsop. He is old now and spends most of his time sitting on the windowsill in the front room contemplating the new office block. His old hunting ground where the mice used to live is covered with concrete, and with only eight lives left he has to be careful!

The contractor's liability insurers, who had already paid nearly £10 000 for repairs to Miss Blenkinsop's roof, were not too keen to meet the vet's bill, which at £85.46 they considered to be extortionate, but when they realized that there was a good chance of recovering a large part of their outlay from other parties, they eventually agreed to effect settlement.

Chapter 12

PROFESSIONAL INDEMNITY INSURANCE

N.T. Pepperell

Insurance rests upon the principle that a risk is recognized and shared with others for the payment of money, the assured being protected from a serious loss or personal catastrophe should the feared event come to pass. The insurers are gambling that the total of all the premiums paid to them from a variety of risks will be in excess of any and all likely claims, plus all operating costs and commissions to brokers. This should eventually leave them with an adequate profit return.

Most insurance is based on the protection of something, some object or some definable risk event for a period of time. The period of policy life is usually not more than one year, professional indemnity insurance being issued for only one year at a time. Its scope is somewhat different in that it attempts to cover the possibility of claims arising against the professionally qualified and professionally registered assured from or out of or involvement in or with a wide and sometimes imprecise variety of work done or services offered. Cover should embrace the provision of professional services or any future or historical liability arising out of 'joint and several' involvement with others. Professional indemnity insurance policy documents are generally written to protect any claims events arising out of negligent acts, errors or omissions. That is within the context of what is understood to be defined as a normal professional service or the duty of care owed by and within that particular profession.

There are many classes of insurer within this class of professional indemnity (PI) insurance business but they do not have a standard form or policy wording. It cannot be assumed that because a policy is called a professional

indemnity policy it will cover all professional risks. Many PI policies are
written to exclude certain types of risk and all the small print has to be read
and understood. An example lies within what is called the exclusions section
which is where the policy document will contain a warning about what it does
not cover. In most current professional indemnity policies, these sections will
include a phrase to the effect that they do not cover guarantees, performance
bonds or voluntary extensions of statutory duty. An example is the signing of
most forms of 'collateral warranty' when requested by clients wishing to bind
their consultants into owing contractual duties to future third parties. These
demands mostly lie outside whatever statutory duty is owed so the voluntary
signing of such documents in respect of work done can and mostly will remove
the insurance-backed protection that would or could have otherwise existed.

Professional liability

To be liable, a person has to owe a duty of care which in the case of the
professional person is held to be more extensive than that of the lay person.
However, the duty of care owed is one of reasonable skill and care relative to
those circumstances, in that situation and for a person of that qualification
and experience, not a duty of perfection. In the case of a contract, the duty
owed is one of strict liability and will be in accordance with the expressed
terms of that contract. The common law of tort is often applied to third party
claims and to legal actions for damages commenced by people not necessarily
party to the original contract. Claims in tort can sometimes be by former
clients seeking to go outside the terms of the contract. We find ever-evolving
legal debates within which lawyers are constantly trying to broaden the scope
and degree of the professional duty they claim is owed. They make their case
in such fashion as to suggest that the damage or injury or loss caused to their
client is entirely due to a breach of or lapse in what they hold out to be the
professional duty of care that was owed. These lawyers often try to imply that
the duty of care owed is one of result or unqualified perfection rather than of
reasonable skill and care. This legal approach to attack is changing the way
that many professional people must now respond to the demands of
professional practice and influences how they must set about arranging the
insurable part of their professional risk.

As a result of the way in which the law is being applied some insurers are
seeking to exclude certain types of liability and claims or at least limit their
own financial exposure. The insurers may claim that they are only insuring
claims derived from definable duties and professional negligence therefrom.
If so then broad claims based on an alleged ill defined breach of professional
duty cannot automatically be assumed as covered under many policy terms
and conditions. Ironically, claims may be derived from a wilful professional
act done in good faith rather than one which was negligent in the sense of
acting carelessly or incompetently. Such is the mysterious beast that lurks in

the shadows to seize upon the good name and resources of the unwary professional.

Obtaining professional indemnity insurance

Before buying professional indemnity insurance you must determine what you are actually trying to insure, to what degree, to what amount and for how long. The insurer will not define these things for you as they see their role as offering terms to cover what you wish to have covered and not to tell you what you should cover. The role of the broker is often confused in that they are not the providers of insurance but are the purchasing agents of those wishing to be insured. They not only have a duty to negotiate the best terms in connection with what has to be insured but also to become involved in any future claims within the life of the policy on behalf of the assured. Brokers are also expected to give appropriate advice where there is the threat of a claim or in the case of the professional person having knowledge of a notifiable circumstance that they reasonably believe is likely to give rise to a future claim. Unfortunately, many of the professional people buying PI insurance do not take enough care to determine whether the broker selling them the insurance has adequate specialist knowledge and in-house expertise in this class of business. If such expertise is lacking, appropriate or even vital advice to the assured may not be given in a professional or timely fashion. My advice is not to use generalists but only insurance broker PI specialists when buying this type of insurance policy.

PI policies are purchased as an annual event and issued on the basis of being 'claims made' policies. This means that a current policy has to be in existence at the time any claim is made or any notifiable circumstance recorded for it to be covered. It is not the policy that exists at the time work is done for the professional services provided that covers any future claim. Many clients do not understand this principle and wrongly believe that if the professional person or firm is insured at the time work is done then they will be secure in the future. The only way this can be achieved is for them to buy a quite separate policy, i.e. 'project insurance' to cover a building for listed and definable defects for up to ten years. This term is the maximum period of time covered by this type of policy. However, such policies only apply to new buildings and to date are largely restricted to non-domestic work like commercial and industrial developments.

Professional architects and other similar consultants must make careful use of prescriptive wording and any accepted professional references when confirming their conditions of appointment to clients. This description should include the scope of duty within legally permissible limitations on the duties owed and in respect of the professional services they are intending to provide. If they do this as a matter of good, as well as safe practice, they will not be so vulnerable to opportunistic claims in future. Care taken in this area should also be beneficial when obtaining new or competitive PI insurance. It will probably result in requests to pay lower premiums than those professionals who are less careful. A carefully written definition of services and implied duty attached thereto is an important limiting influence on any future claims. If claims are based on alleged breaches of professional duty rather than breaches of contract, the degree of liability will be influenced by certain legal case court judgements, e.g. D. & F. Estates *v*. The Church Commissioners & Wates. On this basis it can be argued the duty owed to third parties should be no greater than or will be closely related to the duties agreed to by the contracting parties at the outset. In the absence of such written definition it can be argued that there is duty without limitation and this is where the professional may be at risk of moving outside the agreed scope and protection of the insurance policy. Some insurers will allow less latitude than others if or when faced with a claim due to this type of uncertainty.

In planning the purchase of PI insurance, an important factor for building professionals is the duration time of liability when related to the limitations contained within the Limitation Act of 1980 and more recently the Latent Damage Defect Act 1986. The 1986 Act contains a 15-year liability longstop from the date upon which the or any professional breach of duty occurred. This means that a PI policy must be negotiated so as to cover all work done or services provided historically and to provide current protection for as long as there may be carried forward liability. Some PI policies restrict cover to only work being done in the current policy year. Such policies may still not be cheap but are largely useless in terms of risk protection. However, as a warning, if it can be proved that there was conspiracy to conceal a defect or there was concealment in a fashion held to be fraudulent then the time bar protections to bringing legal proceedings are set aside.

Extent of policy cover

Having decided what you wish to insure, make a sensible assessment of what at worst could go wrong with the work you have done or work you are likely to do. Reflect on what at worst it might cost at current prices to put the problem right if you were sued and found guilty. You should also understand what it could cost you or insurers in legal defence terms to prove your innocence. Armed with your prepared thoughts, you can explain what is required to your selected specialist PI insurance brokers, and get his/her best advice. After discussion the broker may provide you with an insurance proposal form which you will be asked to complete carefully. Also ask to see a copy of the insurance policy wording to which it refers as you must check to make sure that it will cover what you require. You should get the broker to take you through the clauses and technical wording so that you understand it. This briefing session will act as a check to show you whether the broker actually knows what he/she is talking about. If not then go somewhere else as your own personal risk exposure is too important to leave to amateurs. You should not allow anyone else to complete this form for you. Any errors in it could mean your policy is open to being cancelled for non-disclosure in the future event of any claims. If a firm or partnership makes such an application, it should be delegated to a senior and responsible person within the firm but on completion shown to and signed or initialled by all partners as a check. Some insurers faced with a claim are quite ruthless about errors of non-disclosure even when they are innocent. Policy wordings with clauses saying they will be voided for any non-disclosure can be open to being cancelled in the event of claims for quite innocent errors of detail or fact. The 200-year-old law of insurance is *uberimmae fidei* which means utmost good faith. This imposes a duty of full disclosure upon the person seeking to buy the insurance and during the life of the policy to make known to the insurer, usually through the insurance broker, any material fact that might influence a prudent insurer's judgement. If the person filling out the form recognizes that the questions asked do not necessarily cover all the things the person wishing to be insured considers important, then it is in the best interests of the applicant to make known any other material information that might be important. This can include good news as well as any bad news. If a professional firm or partners have been awarded prizes for good work, this may beneficially influence the insurer to offer you a cheaper premium. Armed with this completed proposal document, which is signed personally by the applicant who declares it as a true and honest statement, the broker sets off to meet with the insurer and negotiate the best price and terms. These terms are conveyed to the applicant who normally has a short period of grace to accept or reject them. As soon as the terms are accepted by the assured and confirmed as such to the broker, the person accepting them becomes 'on risk'. This should mean they are covered by the insurance from that date for the annual life of the policy, unless for any mischance there were grounds to cancel it. Clearly, the payment of the premium within an agreed period of time is essential for cover.

The assured will be sent or should demand a copy of the policy document containing what is the agreed policy wording. This should cover any endorsements that may include or exclude items not listed within the printed form. Remember insurance is negotiable and anything you wish to be added to the standard form can usually be purchased at an extra price. This document should be kept somewhere safe and in the event of one of the answers in the original proposal form turning out to be incorrect it is prudent to advise the insurer immediately through your broker and say in writing 'I'm very sorry but my answer to such and such a question has turned out to be incorrect because . . . and the accurate answer is now as follows'. In the event of changing answers you have given in past proposal forms or changing previous answers that will be on record when filling out any new forms for renewals, give a note of explanation about why your answer has changed. In that way the insurer will see that you are being careful, honest, fair and reasonable. It is to be hoped that, if you ever reach a grey area requiring an understanding decision, they will be equally fair and reasonable with you.

In the life of the policy there is a duty to make known to the insurer, immediately it becomes known to you, any material information that may give rise to a claim or influence an existing claim. In any such an event you must not try to settle things without first consulting the insurers through the brokers who will appreciate your candid appraisal of the situation. They will be receptive to any practical suggestions as to how you would like to resolve the matter or contain the loss by the most cost-effective and short time route. This sort of notification should be done immediately by phone once known to you and also confirmed in writing. Do not delay making such notifications as it may prejudice your protection. Following receipt by the broker and insurer, such notifications should be recorded in their claims record book as being accepted and given a number. The claim or notification number should be confirmed to you in writing by the broker and that letter must be kept with the policy document to which it refers. Once a claim is made against a policy it is that policy that will deal with the claim even if it takes several years or more to resolve. Many PI related claims seem to take years or more to resolve after notification as the matters are often complex and the allegations require research by experts to defend or to give a legal or technical opinion. All this tends to mean a flow of letters between the lawyers of the various parties which adds enormously to the cost. Make quite sure your lawyers are conversant with this type of claims situation and have first-hand recent experience in dealing with such matters. Many do not and seem to cause a minor claim to escalate into a bigger one through failing to appreciate an important technical fact early on. Remember lawyers get paid win or lose; it's your money and reputation at stake, so get good value for their fees.

There is a temptation to try to negotiate cheaper prices at each annual renewal of insurance. However, like all relationships, one built over time can be valuable when exposed to pressure and emergency. There are hidden continuity discounts for staying with an insurer for years. Even if there have been no claims recorded, the hidden legal costs of handling any notifications about the possible threat of claims or of serious circumstances can be appreciable and will be absorbed by the better insurer. If not they may well become a bill to be paid by you out of the excess or deductible amount to be first paid by you before the insurers have to respond. One should bear in mind that not all insurers are UK-based and if using a policy written by an overseas company you need to understand what these countries' technical terms mean.

How much to insure for

One difficult question often asked is how much to insure for. There is a simple if crude rule of thumb used by some insurers which is to take the gross fees earned plus VAT in the previous year or last full accounting year of the firm applying for the PI insurance and multiply by two-an-a-half. As an example, fees of £100 000 would give rise to an insured level of about 250 000. This may vary according to the individual nature of the work done by the firm or arising out of demands made by clients which may be carried forward contractual obligations. In addition to this you can insure for an aggregate amount or on an 'each and every' claim basis up to the sum assured which would probably cover all claims below that level if several were made within the same policy life. The terms of that policy need to be read in conjunction with this outline.

There is no statuary obligation to be insured and not all professional institutions demand it of their members in private practice. However, it is advisable to be insured to a reasonable sum with a broad-based policy through a reliable insurer. We live in a predatory society within which many people are encouraged to seek advantage or gain at another's expense. Liability claims for or alleging breaches of professional duty of care made against building professionals by clients, owners, tenants and public are packaged in many forms. They frequently include alleged negligent design advice which is rarely clarified to start with but often turns out as building defects like leaks or roof flood damage which is caused though poor workmanship. They include the occupants claiming that the building does not give reasonable performance relative to their needs which may not relate to the original design brief, for example, the washing of floors with aggressive cleaning fluids leading to the destruction of floor finishes. They include tenants on full repairing leases having to pay high maintenance costs because the original developer instructed all initial contract costs to be cut to the bone. In the absence of a legal life of a building in its trinity of structure, envelope and services, who is to say what is then a reasonable performance if no minimum life in use is defined by clients to consultants at the very first briefing stage?

Liability for professional advice

This book addresses the subject of site selection. If a professional gives advice on which a client intends to rely and this causes the client to purchase a site as a consequence, then if that advice is negligent the professional could find him/herself liable to make good any commercial loss. Site purchase relies on feasibility studies and reports which are often prepared in an unstructured way and can be more damning by what they leave out than what they include. Professionals should remember that reports are issued for only three prime reasons: the professional is giving information upon which the client and others in future may claim to rely; the professional is seeking accurate information in order to demonstrate he/she has considered all relevant matters in preparing an accurate professional opinion; and the professional is seeking decisions or approvals from others on behalf of the client. In the last context undertakings must be careful in their choice and use of words.

Consultants engaged to obtain planning permission must point out that is not within their gift to obtain it but only to apply for it. Ignore this rule and someone like a developer left with a site upon which permission has been refused, finding it worth less than its purchase price, funding the interest on borrowings, may seek to claim to recover the loss. It may well be said that this loss is due to not obtaining planning permission which the consultant undertook to do.

If doing any feasibility study the following guide may help outline some of the critical issues to be covered so as not to be accused of breach of duty and limit future liability.

Make clear to the client the specific matters you have dealt with and state clearly those matters you do not wish to be associated with. Give the client the chance to appraise any report and name its limitations. If clients deem it appropriate they have had due warning by giving them the opportunity to take extra advice or obtain additional information they consider important.

Site feasibility report format

1. Confirm client's instructions
2. Summarize contents
3. Outline client's brief
4. State limitations on contents
5. Confirm any omissions or information limits due to lack of time
6. Confirm if a full measured survey has been done on property or site or not
7. Confirm any structural analysis of property or not
8. Confirm method used to establish site boundaries or not
9. Confirm soil test if made or not
10. Confirm any sketch plan is for ideas only
11. List all other consultants involved in the report
12. Confirm all local authorities involved in report
13. List and confirm all known existing rights or constraints in connection with the site: light, supports, right of access, restrictive or other covenants, party walls, easements. Add any other important considerations. If any such matters have not been checked then declare that as the case. State how the information was obtained and checked. If of dubious origins state that further checks should be made if reliance is to be placed on it. If any checks remain outstanding declare them. Silence may not be golden in liability terms
14. If previous planning refusals or important constraints to a development exist then include them with dates in the report
15. Include any general information of potential interest or likely to influence the scheme: local infrastructure, main centre, transport, shops, topography etc.

Appendix

CHECKLIST OF ITEMS TO CONSIDER WHEN CHOOSING/ COMPARING SITES

Dan Lampert

Appoint a project team to review the following:

The location

- close to road, rail, inland waterway or airfield?
- strategically sited near to the 'market'?
- near source of raw materials?
  - are raw materials sufficient for life of project?
- near to pool of skilled labour for operation?
  - is pool of labour likely to dry up for any reason?
- if in an inner city location will it be attractive to staff?
- is there an infrastructure attractive to staff and families?
- not in an area sensitive to nature conservation
- not where distribution costs will be significant
- not where local taxation is very high.

Getting planning permission

- importance of having all necessary information available before applying

- importance of no ambiguity in application and precise definitions
- planning permission must be assured before land purchase
- how long will it take to obtain planning permission?
- if the project has toxic effluents a technical presentation is needed
- will mitigation and compensation be involved?
- is a public inquiry inevitable?
- any rights of way involved?

Area of land required for optimum layout of project

- ask for plans of property offered to be scaled to 1/2500 in rural, 1/1250 in urban areas
- have transparency of optimum layout using 1/2500 scale in rural, 1/1250 in urban areas
- if area of land on offer is too much, can surplus be sold?
- if land on offer is not ideal shape are additional costs involved and
- will optimum project layout have to be changed?

Ecology and pollutants

- will there be dealings with Nature Conservancy Council or similar?
- any need for forward planning to mitigate bad publicity?
- will public opinion against development be aroused?
- is there need for a public relations consultant?
- should an environmental consultant be appointed?
- disposal of toxic effluents
- any visual problems, will landscaping be necessary?
- any noise problems?
- any social problems?

Ability of ground conditions to support structures

- will the site require special treatment of foundations?
- is there a difficult water table?
- will anti-corrosion treatment be needed?
- if decontaminated land, what treatment is needed and
- what post-development risks are involved?
- is the removal of trees likely to disturb groundwater courses?
- is anything known about foundation problems on adjacent sites?
- has there been a site/soils investigation on this property before?

Contour of land on offer

- if greenfield and sloping is terracing feasible and acceptable?
- where would surplus soil be placed?
- is there any possibility of heave or shrinkage of soil after excavation?

Climatic conditions

- is the locality subject to fog, mists, heavy snow, flooding?
- if so, how many days are lost in an average year?

Access

Road access

- is easy road access essential for the site?
- does access to public highway pass through villages with restrictions?
- do local surrounding roads and bridges need modification?
- is the site likely to introduce or be involved in traffic jams?

Rail access

- would the volume of rail traffic be enough to connect into the main line or
- would the connection have to be made at nearest siding?
- are there adequate handling and storage facilities at nearest siding?

Inland waterway

- are there any existing wharves and facilities available for use or
- will new facilities have to be constructed?

Utilities

Power

- is sufficient power available on site or will it have to be brought in?
- what is known of power interruptions and are they significant?

- will emergency standby power generation be needed?
- what costs are involved in bringing utilities to site?
- what unit rates are charged by suppliers?

Water

- available on site or needs to be brought in?
- is water treatment needed?
- interruptions in supply? need for emergency storage?
- need for a pressurized fire service main?

Natural gas

- available or needs to be brought in?

Availability of skilled labour

For operation of project

- are suitable skills available locally or
- would skilled workers have to travel from outside the area?
- is reliable public transport available or is travel by car indicated?
- are the local wages higher than average in the UK?
- can a shortage of skills be met by training?
- if skilled labour is in short supply would this delay project start-up?
- is there suitably priced local housing?

For construction of the project

- do local contractors have all the skilled craftsmen they need or
- will national contractors have to be employed?
- if the latter, is local housing available or a construction camp needed?
- are there any local restrictions on overtime being worked?
- are construction costs in the locality higher than average?
- is there likely to be an increase in building activity locally which could reduce the supply of labour and increase costs?

Infrastructure

- is the infrastructure adequate to attract and retain staff?
- does it have all the services needed for the project?
- if not, what facilities are needed for the project, at what cost?

Site/soil investigation

- has there been a site investigation on the site recently? By whom?
- is there a need to appoint a qualified site investigation consultant?
- preparation of invitation documents for site investigation
- who will adjudicate and select consultant?
- who will administer the site investigation contract?

Types of foundations

- project team to advise loadings to site investigation consultant and
- to assemble all information on foundations on land adjacent to property (if possible).

Redevelopment of contaminated land

- appointment of a specialist who knows the special techniques required
- need to know exactly former use of land and chemical analysis of ground
- what are the various options available to rehabilitate the area?

The Land Registry

- are the documents available up-to-date?
- have any plots been transferred out of the title of the land?
- who is competent to check registration documents?

Insurances

- will project become a nuisance to neighbouring properties?
- check on insurances of all people and companies involved relative to Latent Damage Act 1986
- if settlement were to occur due to incomplete site investigation, ensure that professional indemnity insurance continues for ten years; also determine what risks are excluded from PI insurance.

The worth of a plot of land

The worth of a plot of land to compare with the asking price seems to depend on what use can be made of the land. For, say, a housing estate which has planning permission the method sometimes used is the 'residual value', as follows:

The market value of the site is calculated as if it were a completed project – all building, roads and utilities say – and from this figure deduct the cost of every item in the project except the cost of the land (e.g. all construction costs, finance charges, professional fees, interest charges, profit etc.); the amount remaining is the worth of the land.

How to find land suitable for industrial development in selected locations – sources

- Recommended land agents in and around desired locality
- Land agents in London and provinces with national properties
- Advertising (through solicitors?) in local and national newspapers and journals
- British Rail Land Bank, c/o B.R. Property Board, Hamilton House, 3 Appold Street, London EC2 2AA
- British Waterways Board, Property and Development Manager, Melbury House, Melbury Terrace, London NW1 6JX
- Local authorities
- Local Chamber of Commerce
- Department of Trade and Industry, enterprise zones etc.; Regional Selective Scheme; English Estates
- Tour of likely areas and consult local planning office for details of owners of suitable properties.

Index